Dear Evelyn,

Wishing you abundant joy and freedom.

With Love,

[illegible] ♡

Freedom Is Your Nature

A Practical Guide to Inner Transformation

By Christine Wushke

PUBLISHED BY INNER SPLENDOR MEDIA

Published by
Inner Splendor Media LLC
4700 Broadway
New York NY 10040
www.InnerSplendor.com

Library of Congress Control Number: 2013911195
ISBN-13: 978-0-9889642-0-4
ISBN: 0988964204

Important Note: The information in this book reflects the author's experiences and opinions and is not intended to replace medical or psychological advice. It is quite common during transformational times for intense feelings to arise. If at any time you become overwhelmed by what you feel, contact a trained professional or a support group. Having extra support for your transformation is highly recommended.

Cover design by Vidura Barrios

Printed in the United States of America

To the freedom of human spirit
and the joy of remembering
our true nature and boundless light

Table of Contents

Preface

I'm a Canadian woman in my late 30s with a son, ex-husband, house, and real job. I don't live in a cave and I've never been to the Far East. Yet since the age of 6, when, spontaneously, I had my first Divine experience and felt the presence of the warmest unconditional love, I've wanted and worked to make that experience permanent. But while over the years I've had a number of similar experiences, they've always vanished after some time, leaving me feeling bereft and near despairing.

Then one day about ten years ago, while studying *A Course in Miracles* and meditating on my inner 'I', I felt a pop, and a liquid sensation started rushing up my spine. It felt delicious, and surprising, for I had no idea what it was. I only knew that the more I dove into my inner 'I', the more intense and ecstatic the experience became. Something in my head erupted, and I felt again that same all-knowing, unconditionally loving presence that I'd first felt at the age of 6. Except this time, the feeling didn't go away. I got up from meditation, dressed myself and my son, Evan, and took him to the park. Everything looked completely different. It was as though I'd stepped into another world. The grass seemed greener and the sky brighter.

Over time, the experience shifted, but it was always with me. I didn't have a formal teacher, but I discovered that the meditation technique I'd been using when the experience occurred was one taught by the great Indian sage Ramana Maharshi and was part of a spiritual outlook or yogic philosophy known as Advaita Vedanta, a form of non-dualism.

At 34, I met Karam, and soon realized that I felt towards him a complete trust as a spiritual teacher. I knew instinctively that wherever I was going, he was the one who would take me there.

One month later, I dreamt I was flying through space, and at some point I realized I wasn't really dreaming at all. I felt a deep sense of fear rise up, and I knew I wasn't in control. I saw what appeared to be a membrane coming towards me, and the fear really gripped me for I sensed that if I hit that wall, it would be the end of 'me'. I tried to resist, but it was futile. I was rushing towards it and there was no slowing my momentum.

When I hit the wall, I popped through it and out the other side. In that moment, everything became still and completely silent. All momentum ceased and I was suspended in space, in a vacuum that was pure and still. After a while I returned to body-consciousness, and when I opened my eyes, everywhere I looked I saw and felt that same delicious emptiness and perfect stillness.

It took me almost six months to realize how significant this shift had been — and permanent. I remember standing in the kitchen looking at my mom and these thoughts I had always had about her just fell away. It was as if all my expectations about our relationship and my belief that I knew who she was and how she should be were erased. I was seeing her clearly for the very first time, and because of this we could be intimate, truly and fully intimate. It was amazing. I began to have the same experience with my ex-husband, my sister, and my son. It was letting people be who they were, with full acceptance and with no judgment. I didn't have to fix them. I only had to love them. And this change of view really did shift the tenor of *all* of my relationships.

Around this time, people started asking me questions and I began to share with them what I'd learned. People reported back that what I had told them had greatly impacted their life for the better, and asked me to share more. I hadn't been moved to talk about my experiences until people started asking me, drawing them out. Which is how, eventually, I came to write this book.

If someone were to ask what this book is about, I'd say: No matter who you are, no matter where you are, it is possible to live in harmony with your world and your own self so that you don't feel your life is a constant struggle. Everyone can do this. I've done it. You can do it. It is your birthright.

So please come with me now and I'll show you how.

Introduction

What do you really want?

I ask this of my clients often: what do you really, truly want? Often I find that when a person sits down to ponder this question, the answer is almost always to be happy, to be peaceful, and to feel well.

We may think initially that what we want is a million dollars or a new job, but when the answer is something of this world, the question I ask next is *why?* Why do you want a million dollars? What would the million dollars bring you, and for how long? Most people would answer that they want the money so that they can have the freedom to not work so hard or to simply be able to rest, relax and enjoy life. What if it was possible to have that same relaxation and peace right now? True relaxation and the enjoyment of life are actually the same as true happiness at the core, and these qualities are fully available to you *right now,* with or without the million dollars.

What that means is, at the deepest level, we all actually want the same thing. What would it mean if we collectively realized that, underneath it all, we all simply desire to be *free, happy, fulfilled and peaceful?* And what if that feeling of happiness and freedom was already inside you, just waiting to be discovered?

This book offers a way to transform yourself, right now, into a contented and peaceful being who is as much Divine as human. I've come to realize that the natural potential of a human being is to be free and to naturally live harmoniously with life. Imagine for a moment how it would feel to discover true happiness and ease in everyday situations. Within each of us is the potential to live freely and fully, and to embrace the panorama of gifts and abundance available in human experience. Within each of us lies the power to choose consciously to move beyond fear into a natural expression of Divine love. Instead of resisting or shrinking back from life, we can choose to embrace it completely and to live in harmony as one human family.

I believe we have reached a point in the evolution of humanity where we are ready to move forward collectively to embrace our full potential, to be more available in relationships, and ultimately more receptive to the abundance the universe has to offer.

What is transformation?

Trying to find happiness in the world is like looking into a mirror and trying to change your expression by touching the glass. If you want to find happiness, then notice where the expression originates. Look to the place in your own self where happiness originates. This is the beginning of transformation.

In terms of spirituality, transformation is a total flip, or 180-degree shift in perception. The shift is moving from identifying yourself as a separate individual cut off and isolated from the universe, to realizing yourself as pure consciousness. Consciousness itself is eternal, indestructible, and unbounded; it is what, in many traditions, is referred to as your original essence. With this recognition of the *essence* being your *true identity*, the *source* of happiness is also revealed to be ever-present and constantly available because it is interwoven with the eternal being that you are. Once this flip in perception takes place, it is clear that you are free, whole, and inherently safe. The experience of wholeness and contentment become a 'default' way of being, and the energy that had once been preoccupied by looking to feel complete is now free. The result is a newfound sense of availability to life as it is and a deeper appreciation for the human experience.

Once the realization of your true nature is rooted and stable, the process of merging or integrating this liberated consciousness with the world of form begins. This change is often experienced as a dramatic difference in how the world is viewed and lived, while the outer appearance of the person stays the same.

To illustrate this let's return to the example above, of a reflection in a mirror. Imagine for a moment that you are looking in a mirror, and your focus shifts from looking at your face to looking at the glass. (Feel free to try this in a mirror.) If you focus your eyes in a certain way, you can put your attention on the glass, leaving your reflected image blurry and out of focus. Hold your focus on the glass for a few moments, letting the reflection have very little of your attention. Now shift your gaze back to your reflection, and hold your focus on your face—notice how the glass seems to almost disappear. This illustrates how easy it is, by shifting our focus, to change the way we see things.

Let's take this exercise a step further and introduce the elements of manipulation and change. Go back to the mirror and see if you can make any alterations to your hair by brushing at the glass. This part of the experiment mimics how perception and change work in the world. Touching the glass does not affect the reflection; if you try to brush your hair, you cannot do so by brushing the glass. This illustrates where the change originates in a spiritual transformation. We transform ourselves by recognizing the source of change itself, not by changing the world around us. Trying to change your outside circumstances in order to be happy is like trying to change your hair by brushing the glass. Happiness can be found at anytime as a felt experience inside your own essential self, here in this very moment. True happiness is unconditional; thankfully, it doesn't need our life circumstances to be a certain way. It can be discovered within you right now. Happiness is our natural state of being, and is already present; right here, right now. All that is required is a subtle shift in focus from your mind and your thoughts about your life, to what is directly felt as your essence within.

As change takes place at its origin, a shift in perception occurs. The shift in focus I will be talking about in this book is an internal shift from focussing on yourself as an isolated separate individual to the very essence of happiness itself.

Like the mirror analogy, when we see the world as outside of us, it appears that we are separate, cut off from it, isolated and alone; that is like having our focus on the glass only. Trying to change our surroundings in order to become happy is like trying to brush our hair by putting the brush on the glass. When we begin to see that the only way to brush our hair is to find where our hair *really is*—not where it is reflected back to us in the mirror—transformation happens naturally. Then we can brush our hair at its origin and see the results in the mirror. When we hold our focus on the felt sense of essence within our own self, at the origin, we recognize also that the reflection in the glass is connected to us and that *we cannot separate it from our own being.*

A transformation of perception is a huge internal change. Instead of the world being viewed as many separate parts, people, and circumstances, it becomes a reflection of our own divinity. Rather than feeling we're a victim of the world around us and separate from it, we begin to see the world is actually a reflection of our own essence. Just as we recognize that our face in the mirror is connected to our very being, through the process of spiritual transformation we realize that the world around us is intimately interwoven fibres of our own essential self. The world around us is the very same essence that is within us.

In short, this book is about transforming the idea that happiness is 'out there' into the experience of moment-to-moment happiness within.

Your guide to inner transformation:

I sat down to write this book after having a dream about flying through the sky with an enlightened master. At one point the master said to me, "We are halfway there; let's land here." We stopped flying and landed on the top of a tall building. Once we had landed, the master handed me three pieces of paper and said, "On each of these papers, I want you to write down some guidance from our journey together. I want you to write to the people who are just beginning to embark on this same journey we are on, but I want you to write it down in three different ways."

The next day I happened to have three Reiki sessions with three different clients. Even though these clients were all very different, the one thing they had in common was that they were each going through a spiritual transformation. All three of these women asked me the same question on that day, and I found myself answering the question based on my own experience, in a similar yet slightly different variation for each.

At the end of my work day it hit me: my dream was telling me that it was time to write down the guidance I was giving my clients in a way that would suit all the different types of people who are going through a similar process. I realized that if I was seeing three clients a day, all going through a similar process, how many people in the world were in the same position and looking for a little guidance? I am guessing that if you have this book in your hands, and you have read this far already, you are already either very interested in, or already going through, a spiritual transformation. I would like to share with you what I have learned so far on my own journey through this profound inner shift in perception in the hope that it may offer insight and inspiration to you for yours. My wish is to inspire you to embrace and embody the full potential of what it means to be Divinely-Human.

Throughout my journey I have kept a journal of my inner observations and discoveries. From time to time in this book I will share these entries to illustrate the various phases of the journey from personal experience. You can identify these journal entries quickly by the indented and italicized text.

Throughout this book you will also notice practical application boxes. These are simple and easy-to-follow experiments and exercises you can use to integrate the suggestions in this book into your everyday life.

If any of the terms used in this book are new to you, feel free to visit the "Clarification of terms" section at the end.

Transformative times

We keep hearing that we are living in transformative times, but what does this mean? Simply put, it means the motive and inspiration for personal transformation has never been higher. With high speed Internet, we as a species have become more aware than ever about what is happening on our planet. For example when the 7.0 earthquake hit Haiti in 2010, word went out immediately and spread through the Internet; within two hours videos were circulating on YouTube, Twitter, and Facebook, and within three hours a simple text message could wire money to the Red Cross.

The state of our world, environmentally and economically, is common awareness for anyone with an Internet connection. Each human being on this planet is wired with a basic survival instinct, and it is becoming more and more clear: if we are going to survive, we have to change our way of being. *Transformation* is really another word for *change*, and whether that change is motivated by a will to survive, or by an inspiration to realize our greatest potential, every one of us has the inherent capacity to change, evolve, and grow. When the motivation to change is heightened, and the resources are readily available, then these changes have the potential to occur very quickly.

The motivation to transform ourselves individually and collectively has never been greater, and it is for this reason that I feel this book and its message are so important right now. Through inner transformation, we recognize that in essence we are already whole, complete, and free. Embracing our essential wholeness is truly the greatest gift we can offer, to humanity and to the planet. Being sustained fully as you are right now means you are free from grasping at the world to fill yourself up. When you don't need anything from the world, or from other people, then everything you do becomes service. As we change from our identification with ideas of lack and separation to a sense of being whole, complete, and connected, we will not only transform ourselves, but by that very act, we will transform the world.

Namaste,
Christine Wushke

The story that begins on the next page is a parable illustrating human transformation. Each aspect of this parable symbolises some part of the process of transformation. Throughout the book, I return to this parable, expanding on its symbolism as we explore the various phases of transformation. I recommend that, as you read, you come back to this story to gain greater clarity and understanding of your own unfolding transformation.

Prologue: It's time

Before recorded time, there was a sacred race called angels. In their travels through the universe, the angels encountered a special planet, Earth. Recognizing Earth as an extraordinary place, the angels wondered if this might be the right location to take the next step in their evolution. For millennia the angels had felt they were outgrowing their present stage of existence and were ready to move forward into a new form, a form called human. After some study, the angels became hopeful that Earth was the perfect place for them to explore this next phase of their development.

The angels made a mission plan and embarked on their new adventure. They flew to Earth in sophisticated inter-dimensional space ships. Looking down on the planet, they realized that, while this blue beauty was indeed perfect, the environment wasn't quite ready for them. The atmosphere was too dense and heavy for the angels' light bodies. They knew that the atmosphere would lighten in time, but they didn't want to wait. The push to grow was strong—they were ready to start *now!*

So, they called a meeting and tossed around creative solutions. Finally it was decided: a group of volunteer angels would go immediately and begin to prepare the planet for their new mission. The angels would create the human form, and the volunteers would merge with it. They would then protect their light bodies in a new high tech space suit. To offset the planet's density, the volunteers would wear the space suit until the planet, and their new bodies, were ready.

Using high-speed technology, this space suit was created from lightweight materials for easy mobility; the face mask was made from a breathable clear glass.

The volunteer angels merged with the sacred human form and dressed in their high tech space suits. Once on the planet, the angels began to explore—and to become enthralled. They began to wander, each going in a different direction.

In time, the space suits seemed cumbersome, and the glass face masks became foggy. The volunteers found it difficult to move or to see clearly. The volunteers became disoriented; they forgot where they were; and—more important—they forgot who they were and why they had come. In the cloudy glass of their face masks, they could see only their own reflections. Looking at the reflection of their own faces, these angels started believing the reflection was all there was. Confused, the angels identified themselves with the reflections in the glass.

Fatigue set in, and with that came a sense of isolation and fear. Separate from each other, each of them wandering alone on a strange planet, they became frightened and began to look for ways to overcome their fears and feel better.

At this point, the angels on the inter-dimensional space ships above Earth were trying to get the volunteers' attention. The time had come: Earth was ready for the angels' mission to begin. It was time to transition from angel to human, time for the angels to make their next sacred evolutionary leap.

The angels on Earth had become lost. They felt fearful and heavy, and as time passed, they felt worse and worse.

One day, one of the volunteer angels slipped and fell into a clear lake. She managed to pull herself out of the water, but, in her wet space suit, she felt even heavier now. She felt utterly defeated. Finding her last bit of strength, she crawled to a sunny spot and collapsed in the grass. When she began to dry off, she saw through the once-again clear glass in front of her face. She could see! Looking around in amazement, she began to remember where she was and why she had come. She realized she had been lost for a long time, and knew that by now, Earth would be ready for the mission to begin. With her new-found clarity, she located the dials in her space suit and signalled to the ship above.

Once she received the signal back that the time had long since begun, the volunteer found a dial inside her suit that enabled her to once again activate her full angelic abilities. After a few moments, the light of her own being shone though the fibres of the space suit, absorbing and dissolving it completely. Now that the atmosphere was ready, the human form and the angelic light could be woven together and united into one Divinely-Human being. The protective layers were no longer needed and they, too, were absorbed and merged into her powerful angelic light. Looking down on her new human form in utter amazement, she started to giggle with the thrill of feeling so light, and alive. She walked around on new legs, and began reaching out, touching the plant life and the nearby water. The sights and sounds were awe-inspiring. She was so thrilled with the excitement of beginning her mission that she nearly forgot the struggle she'd experienced only moments before. It had seemed like an eternity of difficulty when she was in it. Remembering her trials, she began to laugh. She had thought her journey was ending. Now she saw that it had only just begun. The time to be an angel was over, and the time to move forward—to be Divinely-Human—had begun.

Chapter 1

What does it mean to live in freedom?

This pain, this love, this sorrow, this joy; none of it was ever yours; it has never ever belonged to you. Yet all of it, every single moment of it, is what you are. Return everything to the one it all came from. In having nothing, you are free to see that in your freedom lays everything.

People often tell me that the description of being fully human in the story 'It's Time' is exactly what they are looking for, and then they ask, "So how do I get there? How can I find a way to remember my true nature and move through life freely and with ease?"

The first thing I tell them is that transformation is not self-improvement; it is total freedom from the *limitations of the self.* The key is to first realize what you are not (the reflections in the glass), and to then remember the original essence of what you always were, by cultivating *clear seeing.*

The truth is you are already free: transformation is simply seeing through the idea that you are not free, or removing the obstacles that appear to be holding you back. Transformation isn't about shaping yourself into a new and different being; it is about *discovering that you have always been free.* This discovery takes place initially by shifting the focus of your attention from thoughts about yourself to the eternal essence within you that is free right now. Resting in this free essence becomes more familiar and natural over time, and eventually becomes a 'default' way of being. No longer bound by the human experience and identified with it, your humanity can then be experienced freely as the gift it is. As long as we feel bound by our human experience, we experience it more like a prison than a gift. Through this simple shift in focus, what once appeared to be a prison cell transforms into an opportunity and a blessing.

In the introduction, I used the analogy of gazing into a mirror to point to this subtle shift in perception. If you are looking into a mirror and your attention is fixed on the image of your face, it is difficult to notice the glass because your attention is elsewhere. This doesn't mean the glass is not there; it simply means you do not see it clearly. Once you shift your focus to the glass, it is obvious it has always been there, even when it went unnoticed due to our diverted attention. The same is true about eternal consciousness. It is easy to become so distracted by the thoughts in our mind that we do not notice the essence of consciousness that these thoughts arise out of. But once it is seen clearly, then it is easy to find and to recognize as an ever-present and reliable source of peace and happiness.

Practical ways to shift the focus of attention

There are several things we will be going over in this book: the first being cultivation of a *clear understanding* about what is blocking or inhibiting your direct experience of freedom. There are two main obstacles that we will be looking at in this book: the obstacle of seeking a better moment and the obstacle of defending or protecting our self. "When I get that car, I will be happy" is one example of seeking. Looking to the future or the world in order to become happy keeps us preoccupied and away from the happiness that is actually here and now. The obstacle of protecting our self is a habitual and unconscious tendency, stemming from either unprocessed emotional energy or fear of a trauma being repeated.

Once the obstacles are understood, it is a lot easier to actively *see past* them, and to embrace the light and freedom that is available here and now. In the story 'It's Time', the angel falls into a lake and is then able to see clearly through her mask. It is the clear seeing that enables her to remember her *original nature* as an angel, and to move forward to merge that divine eternal essence into the human form.

There are many ways to uncover your inherent peace and freedom; my intention is to give you a few simple tools that you can work with intuitively and then form into your own practice, tailored to your uniqueness. I encourage you to work with the tools offered in this book, but at the same time to *honour your direct experience of transformation,* and find the way that really works for you. It is for this reason that I have shared my personal journal entries with you. As we walk though this process together, I encourage you to write about your findings and experiences.

One of the freedom tools that we will learn to use is how to switch on the light of awareness so that we can see through any dark or unconscious place, and how to cultivate clear seeing. Once clear seeing is attained, it becomes much easier to remember our original nature and to embrace the human experience from the perspective of a pure eternal consciousness that cannot be harmed.

The second tool we will be picking up is how to accept and allow yourself to *be as you are,* and thereby fall into the original nature (or angel self) that you are right now. This approach stalls the tendency of seeking and reaching outside of our self, so that we can see through our distractions (reflections in the glass) to the ever-present source of happiness within.

Lastly, we will be addressing how to *integrate* our eternal original nature into our unique human form, or the process of becoming *freely human.* Through the full integration of our original nature, which is divine, ever present and eternal, with the human experience, they are no longer seen as two separate things. I will be using the terms Divinely-Human, and freely human, interchangeably to highlight the importance of integrating or merging the *two into one.*

It is the recognition of oneness that is the heart of this book. The one consciousness that is behind all thought and all form is what connects us intimately as liberated human beings. Seeing that we have this basic sameness is a constant reminder that no matter what happens on this planet, we are all in it together. Transformation is something that takes place on an individual level as we learn to embrace our own Divine-Humanness, but it also naturally spills over into the collective level, as well. In embracing our humanity, it is only natural to move into a deeper appreciation of the one collective human family. When oneness is embraced, harmony follows.

What is your original nature?

In the story 'It's Time' the angels are symbolic of our original nature. They represent the consciousness that was 'aware' before the space suit was put on, and physical experience began. When the space suit became cloudy the angels 'forgot' who they were and why came to a planet: this represents the process of identification with a separate self. Believing one's self to be separated from the world and others leads to feelings of lack and isolation. Feelings of loneliness and isolation often spark the beginnings of a spiritual quest for fulfillment. The spiritual seeker longs to return to the original state of being and to unite with something higher. The irony is that our original nature has never gone anywhere, and so the spiritual quest is actually a search for something that is always here. Spiritual transformation is a flip in perception from the appearance of separation, to the experience of oneness.

Regardless of disorientation and 'forgetting', the self in the space suit never changes; it was always right there. This metaphor in the angel story points to our eternal consciousness that has merged with a human form in order to have a physical experience and then forgot about its eternal aspects. Getting lost in the space suit (the mind, thoughts, personal story, drama, social and spiritual conditioning, etc.) represents the identification with the 'story of me'.

An important aspect of transformation is a shift in identification from the personal self to impersonal eternal consciousness. The identification with the personal self is like believing that everything is 'all about me'. An example of this is when someone scowls in your direction, and you assume that they have just given you a dirty look. In reality that person may have just experienced a sharp pain in their back, and the expression may have been their response to the pain. When we can shift our focus from the personal story to impersonal consciousness, the expression on someone's face is no longer 'about me'. Instead of taking their expression personally, it can be seen for what it is: another human being feeling, and responding to pain.

> *I had been reading* A Course in Miracles *quite actively for a few years when I had my first taste of this shift in identification. One day I was contemplating one of the lessons which was 'these thoughts don't mean anything'. The exercise that day was to watch a thought arise and then mentally repeat 'that thought doesn't mean anything' for a period of about five minutes. During the course of this practice period I was hit with a sudden inspiration: 'who is the thinker?' And I was suddenly overcome with a deep inner curiosity as if I had stumbled upon the most important question of my life. At some point during this practice a sudden realization hit me that 'I am not real'.*
>
> *For whatever reason the words 'I am not real' seemed to pack a punch, and as this sentence settled deeper, I genuinely considered 'I really am not real'. At that point I began to feel a sensation like liquid moving up the base of my spine. The contemplation of this*

sentence 'I am not real' seemed directly proportionate to how intensely the liquid energy moved up my spine. As I dove more and more into the feeling of being 'unreal', the liquid would rush more intensely.

At some point the rushing sensation became more predominant than the thoughts, as if a loud noise was drowning out all else. The sensation of rushing liquid increased more and more until it was simply all there was. At some point that sensation moved beyond the level of the physical body, as if the rushing was now expanding outward to fill a new and larger parameter. The expansion continued for some time, until it reached what felt to be an edge. As the sense of expansion pushed up against that edge, I felt a pop, and then everything stopped.

As I came back to an awareness of my body and the room, the rushing liquid sensation returned. It felt like a waterfall had been placed in my spine: a very pleasant, almost exquisite feeling impossible to describe.

This state lasted for two weeks; a constant sensation of rushing water in the spine combined with a blissful love lifting me to heights of happiness and joy that I had never known before. It started to become clear over time that I had stumbled upon something that day, something that had always been within me but had been buried in the idea of what 'I am' and was now replaced with a deeper understanding. I realized that the character I had been playing out in my life was not the true 'me'.

Over time the experience faded and became like a subtle background noise, though the feeling of silent happiness 'without reason' was never totally forgotten as I continued on my journey of transformation.

Practical application: Remembering your original nature

- Relax in a comfortable position.
- Become aware of what you are feeling, as well as what thoughts are arising in your mind.
- Ask yourself the question "who is feeling this?" or "who is thinking?"
- Take a few moments to watch the thoughts arise and see if you can detect the exact moment when a thought arises. Ask yourself: where does it arise from? What does it arise from?
- Let yourself fall into these questions for a while until you really get a feel for the awareness that is watching them. That awareness is your 'original nature'.
- Rest for a while longer in this feeling of being simply 'aware' and see if you can remember a time in your life when this awareness was very present with you.

What does it mean to live in freedom?

Let me paint a picture for you: imagine that you are standing next to a chain link fence. On the other side is a giant amusement park. This park looks fun and amazing, and you really want to experience what it is like in there. You look all around for a way to get through the fence: you walk up and down and go all the way around the park; you look to see if you can climb up and over, but there is barbed wire, and it is way too high. You see no doors, no way to get in at all.

You really long to enter and experience the park directly, but there is simply no way in. You are separated from the place you want to get to by a silly fence. As you stand outside, you start to imagine what it's like inside. You develop all kinds of imaginings about it, and maybe even some fear about the scary looking rides. After a while, you notice that there are other people standing around with you. You start up a conversation and talk a bit about the park. Realizing that the people you are speaking with are all stuck outside and no one has been inside, you all start to share your ideas with each other. You may even get into a few arguments, as you compare your different notions of what it might be like.

After some time, a woman approaches the fence from inside the park; she walks up to you, and shows you a door right in front of you. It had been there all along but was disguised. She shows you how to reach through the holes in the chain link and open the latch. You figure out how to unlatch the door and it swings open. You are now able to move into the park, no longer separated from it by the fence. You walk freely and excitedly up to the rides. You are finally able to experience it all, the sounds are louder, the sights look brilliant up close and without the fence buffering your view, you can taste the air and feel and touch everything directly.

The ideas you had developed about the park start to fade, being no longer relevant. You also realize that the notions you had about some of the scary rides were a bit off. They just appeared to be scary from where you were standing; but now that you are riding them, you realize that they are actually quite fun.

Living in freedom means that you are not separated from life in any way. Being liberated from the idea of separation (the other side of the fence) and from all of our conceptual imaginings, we are now free to merge fully with all that it means to be human, as well as Divine. In the amusement park analogy, we become awake to our humanity the moment we step through the fence and walk into the park. Living as an awake and free human means we are not separate from anything, there is no separation between divinity and humanity. Being merged with life means that everything is seen as precious and all aspects of humanity are sacred. With each step towards the park, we merge more completely with what it means to be a human being walking around on a planet called Earth. No longer lost in our imaginings or afraid of what might be, we are simply here from moment to moment.

So what stops us from living in freedom? In the short story 'It's Time', I use the analogy of the space suit to illustrate how we unconsciously protect ourselves from our environment. In that story, the angels want to come to Earth and have the experience of being human, but have to find a way to survive in the dense atmosphere. The space suit is useful at first, but the angels rely upon it too heavily and they forget why they came. This example points to how our behaviours of self-protection become unconscious. We literally forget we are protecting ourselves. After some time, the angels become *identified* with the protective suit, and cannot see clearly through their space suit masks. The angels' view of the world becomes inhibited by the reflections on the glass, which illustrates how we become inhibited by unconscious protective strategies in our lives, ones we no longer need. The reality is that in this moment you are safe. In this moment, you can shine the light of awareness on the mask of old unconscious protections and see clearly and freely.

Practical application: Learning to understand your space suit

- Write a list of three things that you don't like to feel. Just write down the first three things that come to mind; it can be anything from sadness or anger, to the thought of being a 'bad driver' or 'getting fired from my job'. Choose things that genuinely bother you.

- When you are finished writing, see if you can feel the amount of energy you put into avoiding these feelings. How much more energy would you have if your energy was not tied up in avoidance?

The angel story is a metaphor for how the idea of separation creates a 'space suit' in our day-to-day lives to buffer or protect ourselves from the challenges of the human experience. When life becomes challenging, or when traumatic events happen, it is only natural to feel the need to protect ourselves. Later in this book we will be looking at how those protective mechanisms become unconscious over time, and instead of continuing to protect us, they close us off from experiencing our lives fully and completely. Like the space suit, they may start out with a useful purpose, but over time become cumbersome and inhibit our ability to truly connect with others and the world around us. This experience of feeling empty causes us to seek for ways to feel 'full'; turning to drugs, alcohol, unhealthy relationships, emotional eating, or over-indulging are just a few things we use. This feeling of lack is like standing outside the amusement park fence, separated from your life and unable to live it fully and completely, unable to take in all the highs and lows of what it means to be human. Being *freely human* means to be actively present in your life as an unprotected, undefended human being and, instead of bracing back from life, living it fully.

What does this mean on a practical day-to-day level?

One way to describe transformation in practical terms is what I refer to as 'the story of me'. We keep our self separate from life by holding onto a mental story of 'who I am'. After a while it seems safer to hold onto this 'story of me' than to let go and *discover* moment to moment who and what we really are in all its fullness. The images on the glass in the story 'It's Time' are a metaphor to illustrate how we get lost in our *ideas* of who we are rather than diving into the unknown and letting the *mystery* of who we are be revealed to us.

So on a practical level, a great question to ask yourself is, 'What is my story?' *What do I identify with as who I am? Mother, Father, Child?* Do you identify with your career as who you are? What if there is so much more to who you are than your ideas about yourself reflect? Are you willing to dive into the unknown mystery and discover amazing things?

Practical application: What aspects of your personality do you identify with?

- Write down three things about yourself that you identify with. They can be things like 'mother' or 'father', but they can also be things like 'easygoing', 'nice', 'pretty', or 'kind'.

- Try to choose positive things as well as some negative ones. For example, if you choose 'easygoing', check and see if there is also an aspect of yourself that is 'difficult'.

- Be honest with yourself; the more honest you are, the better. The more you can stand back and view an honest picture of yourself with love, forgiveness, and acceptance, the more effective the exercise will be.

Chapter 2

The space suit: Understanding your walls of protection

Where inexhaustible love meets the broken open heart ... that is where true availability lies.

What are the various ways we protect ourselves as people living in a hectic and often stressful world? There are many ways we protect ourselves and many reasons why, though if you peel everything back to a universal level, it comes down to the avoidance of intense feelings and the parts of life that we don't want to feel. Feelings like sadness, anger, hurt, or emotional pain, to name just a few. One way the unconscious aspect of mind (the space suit) tries to help us, is to buffer the feelings—by overanalyzing them, or by projecting a solution into the future. The problem with avoiding feelings of pain or discomfort by staying in the *thoughts* about the issue is that we are trying to solve it from an expectation of a future outcome, when there really is no way to actually know how the future will line up for us. This is like a spinning bicycle wheel that's making no contact with the ground. The more our mental predictions spin, the more energy we use, when the spinning can never solve the problem. The feelings about the problem *are* here and now, and once we are comfortable feeling intense emotions, we can be able to stay present and deal with the problem with a conscious action. This is like a wheel making contact with the ground and being able to move forward in an efficient way.

Staying in our thoughts only keeps us preoccupied and away from the present moment and as a result separates us more from the people around us or the life situations we are in. The problem with avoiding the feelings that are present is that it results in a feeling of detachment, as well as a sense that 'something is missing'. This can be a vicious cycle; feeling a sense of 'not enough' leads to seeking to feel more, but as we open up more to feel connected to life, pain will arise as well. Trying to be open *only* to the positive feelings and not to the 'negative' aspects of life continues to perpetuate this cycle of detachment. The trick to ending this cycle is to be willing to *confront all* feelings that arise and, instead of moving away from them, move towards them. Being freely human means being open to the totality and *fullness* of life. This means finding an inner strength and courage to move through the full spectrum of feelings available to us so that we can live as present, conscious, aware and receptive beings.

Practical application: It's OK to feel what you feel.

- Allow the feeling to be there. Don't try to make it go away.
- Relinquish personal ownership of it. The energy of sadness does not belong to any one person; it simply exists in the universe as a frequency.
- Practice viewing the situation impersonally.
- Act consciously in the situation from an inner space of moment-to-moment presence.

An avoidance tactic is any way (subtle or obvious) of distracting our self from what is happening in the moment. For example, making yourself extra busy, emotional eating (comfort food), or analyzing a problem can all be used to avoid what is simply unfolding here and now. Avoidance tactics can temporarily diminish a feeling of emotional discomfort, but this just means that the cycle will begin again. Feeling disconnected from life leads to feelings of lack; seeking ways to feel whole and complete, we open up to life, but when the painful aspects of life arise, the avoidance patterns kick in once more. This is an ongoing pattern that I discovered in myself, but as I began to see it also in many of my clients, I started to realize how universal this cycle is.

> *One day I had been in a particularly intense bout of emotional pain and distress. I had been working a lot*

with a relaxation practice called yogic sleep and getting messages from the subconscious through dreams. During this time, I called out before bed, 'Please just give me an answer!' That night in my dream I was being chased by an invisible monster. I knew an evil presence was there, but I could not see it. I ran through the house screaming in terror, and came to a room with huge glass windows. On the outside of the glass was a man writing on a piece of paper. He calmly walked over to the glass window and turned the paper towards me. The piece of paper said "THERE IS NO ESCAPE." Several years passed before I actually realized the profound truth of that dream message.

There is no escape.

One day I was sitting in meditation and the emotional pain was very present. The sudden inspiration arose to 'try something different' instead of trying to make the pain go away as I usually did, (with my various methods of fixing or manipulating the feeling). I decided to simply allow it to be there as it was. For a moment the pain increased, and I heard that same inner voice of inspiration say, 'this is the pain of life'. Realizing that this pain was not about me, or even about anything specific at all, seemed to soften and relax something deep inside my core.

As I allowed the pain to be there, without it being about me, it started to diffuse and decrease in intensity. I continued to allow the pain, inwardly saying yes to it, and embracing it in love and understanding.

The results were dramatic; I felt a freedom and lightness for weeks. But after several weeks passed, the pain arose again. This time I again decided to allow it, instead of trying to fix it or escape it. I recognized that this pain was not 'mine', and saying yes to it dissolved it into a feeling of 'just energy'. I felt like I had stumbled onto some kind of ancient secret that day; allowing the pain to exist as it was without bracing against it, moving to fix it, alter it, or change it, was a key to inner freedom. This key seemed to be in the discovery that pain did not belong to me as a person; the pain was the universal pain of life, and had never actually belonged to anyone. In recognizing that this pain was not personal I was simply allowing it to exist as pure energy floating around the universe. Finally the dream message hit home, 'there is no escape:' life and all of its components are meant to be embraced and allowed, not escaped from, removed, or fixed. I learned that rather than trying to escape from an emotion, I could move towards it, I could allow it to be as it was, as energy.

What I found surprising about my own discovery was that the walls of protection and defensiveness began to be seen with a moment-to-moment awareness. As the unconscious walls became conscious, the realization 'I don't have to do that anymore' really hit home. As the walls of protection were seen for what they were, I naturally felt more connected to life and to the essence within everything. Feeling more whole and complete in the simple moments made the movement of 'seeking to fulfill' less appealing. The lessening of my resistance to feeling the pains or discomforts of life seemed to be directly related to feeling more connected to life, not as something separate from me, but as part of my very own being.

Fear and avoidance

Another purpose protective mechanisms play in our lives is to guard us against what we fear the most. These fears can take almost any expression; my fears ranged from being a bad mother to enduring a traumatic death. Living in fear of a potential future is very disempowering. Nine times out of ten, we cannot control what is going to happen, and trying to change the outcome of events or prevent something from happening in the future is like a surfer trying to change the way the ocean waves arise. By putting our energy into managing or changing the waves, we miss the chance to ride the wave and, instead, end up getting crashed around by it. By understanding that the wave is going to rise in its own way, and being ready to surf it as it is, you have taken your power back, and can then take action in the moment from a place of conscious awareness.

Living in fear of a potential 'what if' takes your attention out of the present and projects it into ideas about the future. Again, this is like a wheel spinning without making contact with the ground. Change cannot happen anywhere other than in this moment in time. By learning how to stop, right now, and become aware of what you *feel* in this moment, you can then face the reality of your present situation and learn how to address it in a healthy way.

One way to learn how to 'ride the waves' is by developing a resilience to facing what the fear really is, accessing the feeling underneath it, and bringing it all into conscious awareness. As long as the fears are avoided, they have the power to run your life. The more we face them, and deal with them consciously, the more we can cultivate an inner strength and resilience to meet challenging situations and ride them out with our power and presence intact. Just like a surfer needs to cultivate skill through training and practise in order to surf the big waves, we can learn to cultivate the strength and resilience to face difficult fears and emotions. Once the fear has been faced, addressed, and seen through, it immediately becomes less frightening. By consciously addressing the feeling underneath the fear, you no longer have a reason to run from it. Once you have the resilience and the skill to feel something intensely, and are used to surfing life moment to moment, the future projecting and protecting can fall away on its own.

The problem with guarding and protecting ourself from what we fear, and avoiding the feelings underneath our fears, is that we also end up closing ourself off from connecting to life. Walls work both ways: while they may serve initially in keeping pain out, they also serve as a way to keep love and connection from flowing freely in and out. By developing resilience to consciously *feeling and accepting* pain and fear, those walls can dissolve because there is no longer a reason to avoid life. The benefit to letting go of our walls of protection is that there is also no longer a barrier to loving and being freely loved.

Shrinking back from the pain of life shields out the fullness of a love beyond description; allowing pain to exist as pure impersonal energy reveals a field of indescribable love that always remains. Love itself is too big to be contained, tainted, pushed back, or even made sense of. Everything in existence returns back to this field of love; therefore, there is nothing to fear or resist. Living fearless of the pain of life reveals an ocean of presence that is beautifully and eternally alive.

One example of facing fears came to me in the middle of a meditation session shortly after watching the movie *The Sixth Sense.*

> *I had just finished watching a scary movie and was noticing my own fears of death and dying. Deciding to use this as an opportunity to face the fear, I dove fully into what I was experiencing. This fear seemed to go particularity deep and after a few moments of allowing the fears to come forward, I realized that I was fighting off the feeling of 'I don't matter'. This was the place I didn't want to go, and I saw that I had been fighting it off for some time. Instead of being present with the feeling I was rejecting it in hopes that it would resolve itself. So I decided to just go right into what it would feel like to really not matter. Initially, I felt a little panic and continued to meet some resistance, but I carried on anyway. I had the sudden inspiration to ask, 'What would it really mean if I totally didn't matter?'*
>
> *After a few moments of watching and waiting, I started to feel as if I was floating and expanding. The felt sense of 'not mattering' was losing its old familiar meaning and shifting into something else, something new. All became silent and still, and out*

of the silence these words arose: 'You are already dead'. For a moment it was as if all time had collapsed, all sense of a linear timeline crumbled and all that was left was a space of pure, simple, open, 'here-ness'.

'Already dead' seemed to be the perfect words to trigger this experience of timeless space, which in itself was beyond words. For several weeks I felt like I was walking around as a living ghost; the sense of being 'already dead' was constant. It was as if the fear of this looming future event was now erased, and what was revealed underneath was a deeper feeling of freedom and availability to life. Reconciling the fear of death and the feeling of 'not mattering' that I had been resisting for so long helped me realize that this feeling I had been avoiding was actually the gateway to what I had been longing for. By going to the place I didn't want to go, I was more open to embrace the quality for which I was longing: the freedom to be available to life as it is.

Available to life

Ironically, the experience of feeling 'dead to life' opened a gateway of availability to life as it is. When ideas, notions and fears fall away, what remains but acceptance? Willingness to meet each moment without shrinking back is like approaching life with a wide-open heart. Having faced our greatest fears, having walked through the feelings of deep pain and loss, we lose all reason to avoid life. Availability isn't something you can fabricate, and it isn't something you do; *it is a result of facing and walking through anything that may be in the way.* Walking into the pain of life as frequency, without claiming to own it personally, means that it ceases to be a big scary monster hiding in the closet. It comes out into plain sight to be seen for what it is. When all the monsters are looked at closely and clearly from a place of non-judgment, they can be addressed from a space of clarity and presence.

A wonderful way to practise this clear seeing is what I call the 'I-don't-know practice'. This practice is a great tool to use in times when fear is present or an intense emotion arises. To give one example, think of the present fear or emotion as an imaginary monster in your closet. This practice is a way to ask it to come out of the closet so you can see it clearly. As long as it is hiding in the dark, it is not *seen clearly,* and it is the unseen things we are most afraid of. Be willing to see it with fresh eyes, as if you have no idea what it actually is. Approaching a feeling from the place of 'I don't know' gives you the chance to see it fresh, to see it beyond the element of judgment, to witness it as pure frequency.

Practical application: I-don't-know practice

- Set the intention to feel what is as energy, without assuming that you know what it is, or what it is for.
- Inwardly reassure yourself, 'In this moment, I am safe'. You may notice some defences or protective mechanisms coming up as you relax more and more deeply.
- Repeat to yourself as you dive deeper:
  - I don't know what this is.
  - I don't know what this situation, feeling, fear, etc., is for,
  - I have no idea.
- Notice how the absence of 'knowing' (or assuming) creates a fresh and open space where the feelings can dissolve or be resolved in a real and honest way.

Chapter 3

Courage to be authentically you

Be all that you are, and everything that is will be revealed.

Somewhere along our journey in being human we develop an idea of 'what I should be'. This idea is often very sticky, attractive and alluring. Over time this idea—like the space suit—becomes heavy and cumbersome, because the idea of 'what should be' and the reality of what 'is' rarely align. This misalignment causes an inner conflict; the two opposing forces (what is, and what 'should be') rub against each other, creating friction, agitation and often a deep-seated pain.

This pain and our attachment to 'what should be' create an ongoing cycle of frustration. Trying to get away from the pain by creating new and better ideas of what you should be is a popular solution and one I tried myself for years.

> *For years I tried to fit myself into the mold (like Jell-O) of what I thought it meant to be a spiritual person. I tried to shape myself, squeeze myself into this mold day after day, watching my reactions, controlling my responses, managing my feelings. I would sit and meditate for hours and achieve high spiritual states of unconditional love and bliss. Then I would go back into my day thinking that the mundane stuff was 'less spiritual' than the 'high' I had just experienced on my yoga mat.*
>
> *Over time that spiritual mold I had so diligently squeezed myself into became too containing; it started feeling stifling and untrue. There was little room left for simply being authentic and spontaneous. It started becoming more and more obvious that it was time to re-evaluate my ideas about how I 'should be', and investigate these ideas a little more closely.*
>
> *Through my investigations, I began to see that being real, authentic, simple and spontaneous was more valuable than my old ideas of 'how I should be', and over time I noticed the mold feeling less important, in contrast to the freedom of simply being who I was.*
>
> *I noticed that the notion of 'who I should be' was only a false sense of security to protect myself from the*

> *unknown. I discovered that, while it may seem safe to stay locked in ideas of a person who is definable, it is actually easier to free fall into the unknown and simply not know who you are. What you are is way too big to be defined or contained, and in embracing the 'not knowing' of who you are, at least you are honest, open, and available to each moment of your life. In letting go of the idea of 'who I should be', the real, authentic and effortless being can be revealed.*

Be here as you are, let life come to you as it is, and say yes to it. No matter what shows up in life, remain vulnerable, real and honest. There is nothing to resist, nothing to avoid; trust the strength in you that is infinite.

Cultivating the courage to be as you are

Courage doesn't mean being fearless in the face of a challenge; it means being willing to stand in the center of the challenge without protection. Courage means trusting the inherent strength within you to move through the challenge moment to moment, and allowing the feelings to arise, knowing you are strong enough to feel them.

Often the problem arises when we are faced with a challenging situation and we try to resolve it through our thoughts. This is very much like trying to change the reflection in the mirror by wiping the glass. Courage is being willing to move into the *feeling* moment by moment during any situation, without getting lost in fear-based *thoughts* about it.

During difficult times it is easy to get pulled into thought, believing that worrying about the problem will resolve it. Often emotional energy is high and intense during a crisis, and to add spiralling around in thought is like throwing gasoline on a fire. This is where courage comes in. Courage to be 'authentically you' in the face of a challenge is the heart of spiritual transformation. Being willing to feel what you feel and honour yourself as you are amidst the discomfort is the key to embracing your true and authentic self. The most difficult thing about an arduous situation is the element of the unknown. It feels scary to not know what is going to come next.

Focusing on the feeling, as essence, naturally pulls and connects you to a place of unshakable inner strength. Thoughts about a situation can make everything seem worse than it really is, but being willing to drop deeper into the moment and allow the feeling to have some space will open a gateway to the unshakable reservoir of energy that can then be applied intelligently to the situation.

By simply stopping and allowing everything in this moment to 'simply be', you anchor to the truth of what you are.

> *In my own process of discovery, I notice that an actual shift happens from thinking about a problem to being in the moment as I am. This shift is like changing gears, going from a difficult gear to an easy and free flowing one. In the free flowing space, I see that there is a very fine line between fear and awe. As the anchoring settles deeply into the essence of strength, life is seen from a place of awe and mystery, rather than fear or threat.*
>
> *Over time I have simply accepted that life is always going to be uncertain; we never really know what is*

going to happen next. Because I am free to choose where to hold my focus, the unknown can be experienced as awe or fear. One thing I have discovered though is that when the certainty of the eternal essence is solid, it becomes clear that you are only ever looking at yourself and the miracle and perfection of who you are.

Seen this way, the uncertainty and unexpectedness of life becomes like a roller coaster ride in the dark. Exciting, fun, and mysterious, the ride of the human experience is something to be enjoyed and appreciated, rather than something to be feared or avoided. The ride of life is full of unexpected twists and turns, but this is part of the awe-inspiring miracle that life is.

Worrying about the future leads to a desire to control the outcome of life's events. Energy gets put into preventing pain and looking for certainty or safety in life situations. If the certainty in what you are wobbles, then life is experienced more from the fear end of the spectrum. The jump into the unknown is scary, and uncertainty becomes something to fear or avoid.

The truth of what you are is something you can have faith in—unwavering faith. What you truly are can never be harmed. This is where uncertainty becomes a fun ride. Every turn is a new arrival, an expected surprise; like Christmas morning for a 3-year-old. What is there to fear, when you know what you are? There is nothing to avoid, turn away from or resist. You can trust life as it is; it may take a leap of faith at first, but it is well worth that leap, because what follows it is freedom.

The inspiration to be yourself

Every now and again we meet someone who is an example of what we can become, who shines a light on our deepest potential. There are so many great leaders, teachers, humanitarians, artists, and inspirational speakers on our planet. Sometimes an inspiring person can wake something up in us, ignite a forgotten spark, and remind us of what is possible. When a light is shone into the deepest corners of our true potentiality, we have unspoken permission to unfurl in our own way and at our own pace.

While it is possible for transformation to be sparked by the inspiring example of another person, it is important to understand the distinction between being inspired by someone and aspiring to *be someone else*. The problem with aspiring to emulate someone is that it brings your attention back 'out there'. Like the mirror analogy, it puts the focus on the *glass*, rather than the *origin* of where change should take place. Each human being on this planet is unique and has something of value to offer the world; if we all tried to be like someone else, our gifts and unique talents would not have the chance to shine freely.

I love Michelangelo's *David* and how he explains that the masterpiece was already inside the marble and all he really did was chip away the excess marble to reveal it. This is a perfect analogy for spiritual transformation. Each human being is already a unique masterpiece. The trick is letting the perfect 'you' be revealed by cultivating courage and the willingness to stand undefended in the unknown as the 'excess marble' falls away.

This is the secret to being available to life; it is much easier to be open, receptive and honest with those you love when you are not trying to be someone else. Honouring and accepting yourself as you are is one of the greatest gifts you can offer. When you are comfortable in your own skin, and free to be yourself, you also hold a wordless space for those around you to show up just as they are. This creates a space of relaxation and mutual respect. When people feel honoured as they are, they tend to lay down their defences and allow themselves to also freely *be.* This shifts the energy from an action of *doing* into a relaxation, *an allowing,* and a simply being. Simply being together with loved ones is much more rewarding than trying to step around each other's defences. In *being,* we can really meet each other and find a space of true connection in the heart.

In my own experience, I find the moments of defencelessness and authenticity to be full and complete; the level of my receptivity to life increases the less guarded I am. Receptivity goes both ways—in putting up walls of protection you are not only holding life out but you are also unable to give fully and freely *to* life. The key to releasing protective patterns and defence mechanisms is to bring them into the light of awareness.

Being able to gently observe yourself with an attitude of self acceptance and self forgiveness is the key to undefended living.

> *I remember one particular meditation where I was deeply investigating 'thought'. After some time of looking at thoughts really closely (as if under a microscope) I realized that they are merely fluctuations in a field of silence and stillness. On closer examination, I saw that if I looked at each fluctuation as a curious*

observer (without knowing what it was), all the fluctuations were simply frequency. I saw that everything was either silence, or fluctuating silence; in other words, everything is a variation of one thing. As I got up from my meditation and went about the rest of my day, the realization continued: 'all of life is energy', everything is fluctuating silence.

What struck me as ironic in looking at life in terms of 'all is energy' (and all energy is formless) was that I noticed that any wall I could ever build to protect myself from life would never actually work. There is nothing that can really hold back life; nothing will ever be able to hold out against the energy of life. The energies of life will always be in front of, behind, and within the protective walls.

As I continued to observe life as simple fluctuations of silence and consciousness, I also observed that the energy of life could not be contained or owned. Seeing that I could not possess certain aspects of life and keep out others felt like living as an ocean. Trying to extract those parts of myself I didn't like would be like the ocean trying to cut itself into pieces and move them around. I saw that whatever was resisted would just come back over and again until it was allowed to be absorbed completely into the whole ocean of life that I am.

Practical application: One taste meditation.

- Bring your awareness into this moment, don't try to change anything at all, observe where the 'shoulds' are coming into play. ('I should feel this', 'I should think this way', 'I should be experiencing this', etc.)

- Now STOP, right now, and fully allow everything to be as it is.

Chapter 4

The secret to letting things be as they are

Stop right now, and just let the world be as it is, let everyone and everything happening right now be as it is. Let sadness be sadness, let joy just be joy, let love just be love, let sorrow be sorrow, let happiness be happiness. Let people just be who they are, where they are, as they are.

The power of allowing

The beauty of allowing is in the space it creates. When something uncomfortable arises (either in form, thought, or emotion) the initial tendency is to resist it, fix it, or detach from it. There are so many strategies for getting rid of discomfort. The problem is that none of them seem to work for very long. Fixing strategies are like temporary Band-Aids that we place over uncomfortable feelings in hopes that their discomfort will one day go away forever.

Allowing all thoughts, feelings and emotions to simply exist as they are, gives these energies the space to dissolve, move or deeply heal, according to a natural intelligence. The secret is in allowing the energies to be there, without attaching a personal sense of ownership to them.

To illustrate this more clearly, I will walk you through a short visualization.

Imagine that you are walking down the street and you notice the moon is full. You think to yourself, 'Oh good, I must have done my practice really well this week, because the moon is fully here'. A few weeks later you walk down the very same street and notice that the moon is almost new, so you think 'Oh darn, I must have done my practice poorly this week because the moon is going away'.

It sounds ridiculous, I know, but this is how the mind works when claiming the various energies of life. If we experience sadness and we don't like it, the mind will claim it by assuming that it has done something 'wrong' to make the sadness come. And if joy is present, the mind will claim it by assuming it has done something 'right' in order to bring joy near. By removing the element of personal ownership, sadness can just be sadness, and joy can just be joy, and both energies can be free to come and go, without them meaning 'something about me'.

From here it is not hard to imagine an inner space where all energies are impersonal and free to come and go. It is the claiming action in the mind that causes our struggle with these energies, not just the energy itself. In recognizing this, all energies can simply come and go like the cycles of the moon; in accepting that, we can freely celebrate joy when it is present, and recognize that when sadness is present it is fleeting, and will pass as surely as the moon will once again become full.

This radical acceptance and *allowing* the constant variations of life opens a space to reveal an inherent and subtle hum of simple happiness and being-ness that doesn't come and go. This subtle happiness or peacefulness *remains present* as a backdrop against which all other fluctuations arise and fall. This silent backdrop is something that *can* be relied upon to be ever-present.

When we resist what is, it pulls the focus of our attention to the fluctuations, and if in that moment we feel *defined* by a particular fluctuation, our attention becomes locked there, so to speak. To *allow* the comings and goings to simply come and go without attaching a personal meaning to them, frees our attention and loosens our focus to be anchored in a feeling of simple 'here-ness' and acceptance of what is.

Like the example of the moon, when we recognize its nature is to orbit in cycles, we can see that those cycles are not caused by us and our attention can be free to see the sky that is always there. We can then appreciate the different phases of the moon as an observer. We can see the sky *and* the moon, the changing *and* the changeless.

What about times of challenge in our life?

When challenges are faced from a place of *acceptance,* the tendency is to drop into a present moment appreciation of *essence,* rather than 'over thinking' or dwelling on the problems. Feeling the essence of this moment by dropping into the breath connects us to a reservoir of ever-present strength that nourishes us in the toughest of times. It is important to note, though, that being as you are does not mean forcing a smile or invoking a positive attitude when that is not real. Being as you are means meeting this moment with total willingness to face, and be really honest about, what is naturally happening. If you are going through a tough time, and you feel sad, then just be sad. Let the sadness or grief have total permission to exist as it is. That way the sadness is given room to be free. If changes do need to happen, then they will happen organically, and unfold according to a natural intelligence. The problems arise when we try to force the sadness away, or to dwell on the situation mentally. During these times, the best tool you can use is the breath. The essence of eternity is always in the energy within the breath, it can be found in any moment, and it can feed you the strength to get through anything.

Touching again on the story 'It's Time', an example of the ceaseless nature of eternal essence is to recognize that the *angels never left.* Even when they were distracted by the weight of the space suit and preoccupied by their reflections, the essence within the space suit was *never absent.* The original essence within the space suit was also not harmed or damaged during the journey of forgetting that each angel undertook. The reason *allowing* is such a powerful tool for transformation is that it shifts your focus of attention from the energy of fixing, manipulating, or changing the reflections, to the original essence within that has never left you.

The permanent and impermanent

There is a place where the impermanent meets the permanent; both qualities are naturally occurring, and are natural aspects of life. Where we get into struggle and discomfort often is in confusing the two. When we hold onto a fleeting idea, or an object in form, in hopes that it will become permanent, we are destined to struggle. We will inevitably lose everything impermanent; there is no way around it. The permanent, lasting, and formless realm of causeless love and stillness is never going anywhere. No matter what happens within form, it will always remain ever present and untouched, just like the sky is untouched by the phases of the moon. Knowing this, we can put our faith in a ceaseless and dependable kind of happiness, one we know will always be there for us.

To see clearly that life is fleeting, and that all ideas and all form come and go, whether we enjoy them or hate them, makes us free to appreciate life as it is.

I was once given a teaching in a dream that helped me understand the distinction between the permanent and the impermanent. The understanding of this dream enabled me to embrace life as it is. It showed me that all of life is transient, and I can be free to enjoy the ups in life without grasping at them, and recognize that the downs in life are also temporary and so there is no need to try and make them 'go away'.

This dream took place during a particularly challenging phase of my life; I had gone to bed one night feeling hopeless and drained and fell asleep in a state of despair and exhaustion.

I had a very vivid dream that I was dead. In the dream there was someone beside me that I couldn't see, but I could hear a voice and feel a loving presence. I remember feeling really sad and full of remorse that I had died, and wishing that I could go back to Earth, if even for just two minutes.

The voice beside me offered to fulfill my wish, and sent me back for two minutes. In a blink I was dropped back down to Earth in my familiar body, but surrounded by totally different circumstances. In this new scenario I had just found out that the love of my life was having an affair with another woman, and I was feeling heartbroken and alone.

Elated with being back, I didn't care about the 'scene' going on around me, I felt relieved and grateful just to be back. Knowing my two minutes would be up soon I soaked in every precious second of heartbreak, sorrow, betrayal, and loss.

After getting pulled out of this scene and back to the 'dead' state, I asked again if I could please be allowed to go back for just two minutes more. The voice agreed and I was allowed to go back.

This time I was dropped into yet another totally different scenario. In this one I was happily married but we were going bankrupt and losing everything we owned. Knowing that the two minutes were fleeting, I soaked in every second of financial distress, worry, and uncertainty.

Once more I was pulled out, floating in deadness with the loving voice. Again I asked to go back, and again I was given that wish.

This time I became aware of an interesting time distortion. In the scene around me everything was falling apart, I was feeling the impossibility of 'holding it together'. Knowing the two minutes would end soon I drank in 'falling apart' and the feeling of losing control. I noticed that what felt to me like two minutes was different than the time line playing out in the scene around me. Hours were racing by in the situation around me, while my two minutes were slowly ticking by.

At some point I became aware that I was dreaming and a very lucid thought, 'OK, you have made your point', shattered the dream. I found myself lying in bed, staring at the ceiling. For a few minutes I drank in the sensation of being alive, really alive. I drank in what it meant to be human, and the sweetness of all the things we experience here.

Being able to see clearly the distinction between what is fleeting and what is permanent enables us to drink in life as it is. It offers us the space to remember that a human life is transitory, emotions come and go, human experience is so very brief, and yet, right behind it there is something so powerful, yet subtle, something ever-present that doesn't change. That backdrop can be noticed in any moment by looking at *that which is noticing the comings and goings of life.* The awareness that notices is the same as your eternal essence. That awareness is ever present and can never be harmed in any way. This simple recognition opens up the space for allowing all life to simply be as it is. Just as recognizing that the moon's cycle will change while the sky stays the same. This gives us the freedom to appreciate the moon's presence while it is full, and the absence of the moon when it is new.

Understanding impermanence teaches us that to cling to the changing brings about more struggle, and to try to manipulate aspects of life that we don't like is as futile as trying to push the ocean's waves. Everything within form will rise and fall like waves on the ocean. Allowing life to come and go in this way brings about an inner freedom to appreciate what IS right in front of you, here and now.

Can I control the outcome of events in my life?

This is a question that I get over and over. What about control? One thing I have noticed is that the notion of 'I am powerless' or victim-consciousness can easily be bought into as another protection mechanism. To me this is a very important distinction to be made on the path of transformation. When there is a deep recognition that the waves on the ocean cannot be manipulated, it often comes with the wisdom to also see that the big waves can be surfed. Each person needs to recognize this directly and in their own way. To say that the waves are not controllable as an excuse to stay stuck in a victim mind-set (as a protective mechanism) is the same as letting yourself be crashed around by the waves over and over.

By rooting deeply in your inherent quality of courage, you can learn to let go of the victim or 'poor me' protective mechanism, and dive into that ocean like a surfer would. While you cannot make a big wave smaller, or a small wave bigger, you can empower yourself to learn to surf the waves that are in front of you.

Again, the freedom is in recognizing that the moments when there are big waves—when emotion is running high or when the pain is intense—are fleeting. Eventually all waves subside, no matter what their size or intensity. To live defencelessly, and freely, is to recognize that the big waves are opportunities, treasures to be seized, not problems to fix or run from.

When we live like a surfer, we can see the moments of pain or intensity as the greatest of treasures. With our focus running high in the here and now, there is no time to think or find a way out because we are too busy surfing the wave, letting it take us in, straight to the heart of the moment. When the big waves are accepted moment-by-moment, breath-by-breath, we can appreciate their power and potential to take us to a placeless place beyond fear, into the timeless realm of the heart.

What are you in control of?

At any moment in any day, you can empower yourself. Living defencelessly isn't about allowing your self to be victimized or crashed around by the waves of life. Being freely human means being fully available to life as it is and allowing life to be as it is. This also means embracing the natural intelligence that is within you. This natural intelligence will always guide you to exactly where you need to be and align you with the people that you need to be around.

It is our moment-to-moment conscious choices that allow us to embrace the full human experience. The freedom that is your birthright is *already* present within you, there is nowhere else it could ever be other than right here and now, and no one can change that. What we can control in each moment is where to hold our focus. When we hold our focus on old ideas or mental strategies of protection, we remain distracted and unable to see clearly. When we learn to cultivate courage to be undefended and open to life as it is, we see that it is safe to really be 'all here' and embrace our life and humanity. In other words, we do have control over whether we want to think about life and watch it from behind a fence, or whether we want to *live life fully*.

Bringing the power of allowing into your whole life

Bringing the power of allowing into your daily moments is really where the rubber hits the road. One thing I emphasize in my classes is that meditation is not just about taking twenty minutes to sit on a yoga mat and be still; meditation is about making peace with your life. This is not to say that taking twenty minutes a day to sit and be still isn't valuable, but even more valuable is taking those twenty minutes and weaving them into your entire life, every single moment and interaction with it.

Think of this as a marriage: the wedding day is an important part of the marriage and does have its value in the big picture, but it is the daily life thereafter that is really important. If we look at a marriage from the perspective of its totality, then every daily encounter, every experience shared, and the way we learn to live in harmony with each other is really at the heart of the marriage. To hold all your attention on the wedding and not on the actual marriage that follows does not give the full picture. The same goes for transformation. Some people have awakening events or peak experiences that start them off on a journey of transformation. But the transformation itself happens little by little and unfolds day by day. The peak experiences, awakening experiences, or meditative experiences that happen in your silent meditations can be seen to be like the wedding: they are important, but not as important as the moments that follow.

Likewise, some people are looking for an event or a particular experience to happen to them that will begin an awakening or a transformation process. It is a common distraction to become so fixated on a particular event that we don't realize that the process is already happening *now.* Just like in human relationships, two people can live together with a common law status without ever having had a wedding, and yet all the important stuff is there for it to really be a marriage. If we put all of the importance on the event level (the spiritual or mystical experience) rather than the daily living level, we can get distracted. The most important aspect of transformation is how it affects your whole life, moment by moment.

Making peace with your whole life

The great thing about allowing is that it can easily be woven into your entire life. It is simple and easy and only takes a few moments. All you need to remember is one word: *stop.* Stop right now, and allow this moment to simply be. This can be done anywhere, at any time, in any situation. If you are driving down the highway and a driver cuts you off, just internally stop and allow the situation to be as it is. This doesn't mean you will not act accordingly, and move your car to a safer space, but it does mean accepting that you cannot change how another person is behaving. The trick is in not taking their behaviour personally. Whatever is arising in front of you is your wave to surf, it may be a situation, or an emotion, or even a thought. Take time each day to watch life arise, and let it be as it is, feel what you feel, and don't personalize it.

Let me paint for you another picture. Imagine a glass bottle sitting in a pool. The glass bottle is filled with red food colouring, and the pool is filled with clear water. Let's say the red food colouring is the emotion we call sadness. The glass of the bottle is the claiming mechanism or the idea that it is 'my sadness'. The water in the pool is the source of all energy and emotion. As long as the sadness is held in—by wrapping the walls of 'my story' around it and trying to protect ourselves from it—it will stay intense and circulate inside the bottle.

When sadness is present, the natural tendency is to think 'how can I get rid of this?' but the very notion that it is something to be gotten rid of strengthens the glass that keeps it contained. Trying to 'get rid of it' is another way of claiming ownership of it; *it is not yours to get rid of.* The recognition that sadness itself is simply energy and does not belong to you personally automatically melts the glass. As the walls of defence and protection melt, the red food colouring diffuses into the pool. It is not gone, but merely returned back, or diluted by the source that it came from. The relinquishing of personal ownership of sadness allows the sadness (as energy) to diffuse and dissolve on its own. In this way, sadness is not a problem to be fixed but simply energy belonging to the universe that got contained and trapped by a notion that it belongs to 'me'. Allowing sadness to exist, allowing it to be as it is, without identifying with it, allows the essence of sadness to return to its source.

The next time you notice an energy arising like sadness, hurt, or anger, work with allowing it to exist as something belonging to the universe, no different than the moon, and watch how quickly it dissolves back into its source when there is no personal story to contain it.

Applying the 'allowing' practice to the emotions and energies that arise within you helps you to develop resilience to all emotions that arise and subside within the human experience. With a little practice it is seen that emotions are not a problem, and the more comfortable you can be with accepting and diffusing your own emotions, the more comfortable you will also be with the emotions arising in others. It is so much easier to allow other people to be as they are and allow them to feel what they feel, once you are comfortable and at peace within your own self. The beauty of this is that the more the people in your life are honoured, exactly as they are, the more it gives them silent permission to make peace with their whole life as well.

Practical application: 'Allowing' practice.

- Feel it without owning it.
- Feel it without knowing what it is.
- Feel it without knowing what it is for.
- Allow it to be felt fully in every cell.
- Allow it to be felt so deeply that you no longer have a division between 'you' and 'it'.

Chapter 5

Relationships

The human experience can be painful. Life bites, stings; difficulties arise; and sometimes we try to avoid or escape them. We are human. It's a scary ride at times; and yet we have within us a capacity for strength and courage beyond measure. Beyond all the thinking about it or the philosophizing about it, do we dare to meet one another in raw, open honesty? Do we dare to be fully human and real with the ones we love?

The people in your life are on a unique and sacred path; each and every one is a work of art, a divine mystery. We can't always know why people do what they do, or why things are playing out the way they are. But we can always honour their path, respecting its uniqueness, and trust the way it is, is for a reason. Everyone in your life right now is there for a reason; each relationship is an opportunity to soften our hearts, change our lives, and inspire us to grow.

When we honour each person's sacred path and let them be where they are, it automatically opens our heart. It gives us permission to be truly touched by them and to learn from them. It gives us permission for this moment to be full, and for the fullness of this moment to be absorbed, to penetrate deeply, and to evolve in honesty.

This open-heart space is the space of the sacred, where everything can be seen for what it is. In this space there is no loss because there is no distance. There is no death because there is only the pure aliveness of what you are and always will be. And it is in this space that love can simply glow, for no reason, with a light that can illuminate even the deepest darkness and never be extinguished.

Separation projection and oneness

> *One of my most fascinating discoveries in returning to wholeness was discovering my own reflections, and how I would superimpose these reflections on the people around me. I discovered this in my relationship with my son. When he was little, I felt very insecure as a mother, inadequate, and I had a very deep fear of being a 'bad mother'. Part of the 'story of me' that I discovered on my journey was a much ingrained belief that 'I am not enough'.*

The idea that I was not enough was part of my 'reflections on the glass'. When my focus was held on that reflection or that idea, it was all I saw. The idea 'I am not enough' was never the truth about what I really was, but because I believed it and held my focus on it, I would then see that reflection superimposed on various situations in my life. An analogy to describe these superimposed projections would be holding up a blue transparent glass and looking at the world through it: all of a sudden everything is blue. Everything you look at then takes on the blue quality of the blue glass, and the things you are looking at in the world reflect back many different variations of that blueness.

For me, 'I am not enough' was my blue piece of glass; everywhere I looked I would see a variation of 'I am not enough' reflected back. I continued to buy into that idea and held my focus on it as if it were the truth. The reflections back also seemed to confirm this idea, and 'prove' it to be true.

One of the main places where I began to see through this belief was in my relationship with my son. When I would take him to the store and he would cry, I saw that as proof that my notion was correct. I was personalizing his crying and projecting the idea of 'I am not enough' onto his behaviour, and because this superimposition was unconscious, it happened over and over again.

When my own spiritual transformation began to happen, a lot of unconscious behaviours and ideas came into the light of awareness. One of these was 'I am a bad mother', and part of how this idea survived as a defence mechanism was that I had been perpetually avoiding any feelings associated with 'bad mom'. When I began the practice of walking into these feelings without personal ownership there was no longer a wall of fear separating me from the feeling, and trying desperately to keep it out.

What I noticed was that I was so afraid of feeling 'bad mom' that I would then project onto my son the opposite; he had to simply always be a 'good kid'. I had been putting pressure on him for years to be a 'good kid' for all the wrong reasons. I wanted him to be a good kid because I had a strong aversion to feeling the energy of 'bad mom'. Not only did I have walls of fear built up around that energy but also deep shame. In walking right into the energy of my fear, and ***allowing*** *it to be held in the arms of love and conscious awareness, the energy was released. Now that I felt confident and free to feel the energy of 'bad mom' without attaching it to my personal story, I could let the pressure off my son, and just allow him to be as he was.*

What I noticed in the following months was a deep relaxing and settling into our relationship, and my rediscovery of who he really was as a Divine-Human on his own sacred journey. Instead of needing him to be a certain way so that I could avoid my own feelings, I embraced my inherent courage and allowed the energy of 'bad mom' to simply exist and not be part of 'the story of me'. No longer claiming ownership of these energies enables us to clearly see them as they are.

Now I see that I can feel 'bad mom' energies sometimes, and 'good mom' energies other times, but neither of them is what I am because what I am is not limited to a set of ideas. Now my son is also free to simply be his authentic self. And he is free to feel like a good kid some days and a not so good kid on others, but neither of the two is what he is. This way he is also free to unfold in his life the unique gifts and abilities that are natural and spontaneous to him, instead of being molded to my ideas; he can emerge as he really is without a particular expectation.

Beyond the story, who am I?

To touch again on the space suit analogy, when we are weighed down by the suit and trying to see through the cloudy glass, the reflections we see are *assumed* to be what we are. Bring to mind what you associate with yourself. Let's say it is something like 'mother', 'teacher', and 'easygoing'. Those qualities are all fluctuations of consciousness. When they are moving around on the screen of the space suit and *focus is held tightly on them*, they are like the red food colouring in the glass bottle. On the inside of the glass, these fluctuations appear to be all there is. When the glass is removed, these fluctuations still occur in consciousness as potential qualities and energies to be experienced in the human adventure. When these qualities are seen *freely* without personal ownership or containment, they are like strands of potentiality dancing on a screen of our awareness.

A beautiful visual to describe these frequencies is to imagine the northern lights dancing in the sky. Imagine that each colour of light is a potential quality, flavour of energy, stream of wisdom, information, or aspect of life that can be experienced in any moment as part of the human reality. Imagine that the frequencies of 'mother', 'teacher', and 'easygoing' are floating past you like a display of northern lights. If you keep your focus loose and watch them all flickering around you, you can see all these energies as simple potentiality. When we see a single frequency as the *sum* of what we are, and we define ourselves by a piece of the whole, then it would only be natural to feel contained and limited by this definition. When we stand back and soften our focus on energies, seeing them as free flowing and unfixed, it is only natural to feel that same freedom within ourselves. When we can see the essence of 'mother', 'teacher', and 'easygoing' as energy, the labels of those energies fall away, and our associations, aversions and preferences to them are seen as unreal.

When we stand back without the space suit on, and view life as fluctuations in consciousness, we can let the fluctuations simply be as they are; knowing it is 'not about me', we can feel into the essence of all energies and recognize that at the core they are all woven from the same fabric, they are all variations of one core essence.

The one essence is what all of these fluctuations arise out of, and that same source is to what they are returning. And this essence is also what you are. Even in this moment you can feel the essence of you, beyond any label or definition, as a felt sense of simple 'here-ness'. This felt sense of simple presence or just *being here* is your very essence. That essence is the eternal, the infinite, the limitless, and the Divine. When we can feel into that essence within us, and feel that everything is made up of that one thing, we can really recognize first hand, *that all of this is what we are.* This simple recognition of oneness keeps us connected to all things rising and falling in the field of consciousness.

Life will always be life. Feelings will always come and go. Sensation will always come and go, strong some days, weak others. Challenges will continue to show up in various forms, spin themselves out, and then resolve themselves in some way or other. Good times will always show up in various forms, live out their life span, and die. Life is fleeting, every moment precious; it is a whole beautiful miracle all by itself.

When we recognize that everything we see, feel, touch, think about or interact with is a variation or fluctuation of the one essence, it is much easier to honour the person who is standing in front of you. This does not mean that you will start to like everyone, or let people get away with abusive or inappropriate behaviours, but you will see that, at the core, this person and you are actually not different. The consciousness of the person you are with is the exact same consciousness that is reading these words right now.

The challenging people in our lives

It is much easier to see and experience our interconnectedness with the people in our lives whom we love and hold dear, those people who care about us unconditionally and hold us up when we feel low. It is much harder to apply *allowing* towards people who annoy us, bully us, challenge us, or exhibit abusive and unkind behaviours.

When I am in a situation where I am faced with a person who is triggering me or treating me disrespectfully, the first thing I check in on is my own inner space. One thing that has really helped me is an analogy that goes like this:

Imagine that you are standing in a penthouse looking out your window at the street below. On the street you see a man robbing a woman and snatching her purse. You feel the pull to go and help her, but you can't seem to figure out how to work the elevator door. You are stuck on the top floor and unable to help the woman on the ground. If you could only figure out how to work the elevator, you could get down to the street level, and actually do something.

In this analogy the penthouse is the mind, or more specifically, unconscious thoughts. The street is the actual situation that is happening in front of you in this moment. And here is the key; the elevator is *the feeling;* the energy, essence, or emotion present in the moment.

Staying in the penthouse means being unable to do anything effective in the *present* situation. Or another way to put it: if you are too busy thinking about it, you will never be able to act effectively. That is not to say that all thoughts are wrong or to be gotten rid of, but it comes down again to a shift in focus. It doesn't mean we have to bomb the penthouse to be able to help the woman on the street, but we do need to actually *be there,* standing on the street, in order to address the situation.

Shifting focus to the *essence,* the energy, or the felt sensation in the body, is a way to anchor to the present moment. That shift in focus is like putting both feet on the elevator floor and taking it down to the first floor. Being fully present to this moment

NOW, means action can take place in an effective way; the situation can be handled in a practical and down to earth manner. Moment by moment you can walk down the street and if something needs attention, you act, and if something does not require action then you can relax and observe. Everything is very simple from the street level; from the penthouse, everything is complicated because our thoughts cannot actually *do* anything.

In a challenging situation with a partner or family member, the best thing you can do is honour them as they are, and allow yourself to feel what you feel. As you honour them, recognizing that they are at their core the very same essence, you are also honouring yourself.

Another look at defences

Another way to look at relationships is seeing each person in your life as a gift, wrapped in paper. The paper is their defences, their protective mechanisms, and their unconscious behaviours. If we stay focussed only on the wrapping paper, or the particular behaviour that is challenging us, we don't get to look deeper inside them, to enjoy the gift that is being offered in the moment.

When our focus is on our own unconscious thoughts, or on the other person's unconscious thoughts or behaviours, we end up stuck on the surface unable to see deeper. When we shift focus to what is *behind the paper,* to the essence underneath, we recognize that we are really looking at another version of our own self. If we were to hold each person in our life as if holding a gift wrapped in paper, knowing that a most amazing jewel was inside, it would be much easier to approach the situation with the patience and presence needed to meet the challenge and deal with what is happening in present time.

When you honour the other person and give them space to 'be as they are', they can emerge from the wrapping paper, beyond your expectation. They are free to be the full and empowered being that they are. Just like with Michelangelo's *David*, when the marble was chipped away, the statue emerged; when you see past the wrapping paper and honour the essence underneath, the masterpiece the other person is can emerge.

Often the reason that we want to change someone or don't like them is because we are seeing our own reflections superimposed on that person. In other words, they are reminding us of an aspect of ourselves that we have not been willing to look at. This is another reason why the 'allowing' practice is so beneficial. The idea of 'fixing' someone is usually a direct result of not being comfortable with your own feelings.

One way to describe our unconscious tendencies is to try to see the nose on your face. If your nose is something you are interested in looking at, then a mirror would be a great way to see it clearly. On the other hand, if you have no interest in looking at your nose, then a mirror would be irrelevant. The aspects of our self that are unconscious are not easy to look at directly, just like the nose on our face. It is really helpful to have a mirror to look into, so that you can see more clearly and directly. Once we begin to understand the importance of seeing ourselves, then mirrors become valuable.

For example, let's say I meet a person who has a tendency to bully others. When I am around this person I feel upset, hurt, or angry. In this example, the bullying behaviour is the nose on my face; this is the quality inside of me that I cannot see without a mirror as long as it is unconscious. In this example, the mirror is now the opportunity to look at my own 'nose', (the unconscious idea, behaviour or belief) and bring it into conscious awareness. First I would practice allowing, and let myself feel the hurt or the anger until it diffuses by not personalizing the emotion. Once the emotion is clear, I would look for any places in myself where I bully others, or bully myself. Once I see that I do have a tendency to bully myself, or bully others, I can bring that to the light of conscious awareness and choose to love myself anyway. Now that it is fully conscious, I can also choose to let that aspect of myself go, or to embrace it. As long as the behaviour is unconscious, there is no choice because it cannot be seen.

Once it is all present, clear, and conscious, there is a choice. In this moment I can choose to not bully myself, and in making that conscious choice I have also taken my power back. Now that my attention is in the present moment, and I am in my own power, I can address the behaviour called 'bully' from the 'street level'; from a place of presence and moment-to-moment awareness, I can meet the situation head on and deal with it appropriately.

Once we recognize that the person is a mirror and accept it as an opportunity to embrace and love our whole self, it becomes clear that the mirror, in and of itself, is neutral: our discomfort comes from our own rejection of an aspect of ourself, not from the mirror. At this point things can be seen clearly for what they are, and I am free to sit with the mirror, or not sit with the mirror, but either way it will be the result of a *conscious choice.*

One thing I have noticed in observing people as mirrors is that I am free to appreciate them as they are, because my energy isn't tied up in trying to change them; now they can be met and honoured for the unique human beings that they are. I have also noticed that in doing this, the behaviour that was once triggering me also changes. When a person is genuinely honoured just as they are, and met with a deeper appreciation, they are given the permission and inspiration to bring their own unconscious tendencies into the light of awareness as well.

Challenging situations:

Challenges cannot be resolved from the level of unconscious thought or reactive behaviour; they can only be faced head on from a place of clarity, willingness, and receptivity. In this way we can really meet the people in our lives and offer them our presence, availability, and the deeper appreciation that they are looking for. This way, you are open to being shown what life is really offering and you can take time to see and appreciate the gifts being offered in every situation.

I have noticed this teaching yoga to children. Sometimes the energy in the room can get 'out of hand', and the environment becomes chaotic. These are moments where firmness on my part is very appropriate, but when it comes from a place of clarity and respect the children know it, and the firmness is respected. They can also tell when I am projecting, or trying to 'fix' them or the situation due to my own discomfort. Children can often be the clearest mirrors. When I am clear, conscious, and present with them, allowing them to be as they are and really appreciating them as a unique Divine-Human, the firmness is often respected right away without a fight. When children are met with a deep appreciation and an honouring of their uniqueness, they can be nourished to the core; feeling seen and accepted gives them the space to relax into themselves. When thought is clear and conscious, focus can shift from trying to force a change to happen in another person to *allowing* a change to happen naturally. If change in a situation needs to happen, it will have more space to occur if you allow it than if it is forced.

> *One thing I have found effective in the face of conflict in relationships is to allow the person to be as they are, or to honour their point of view instead of fighting and opposing it. If a loved one is feeling angry, resentful, or hurt and they are saying hurtful things, I will internally honour what they feel before I speak to them. Going into the feeling, whether it is what I feel in my body or what they are feeling in their inner space, doesn't have to be two separate things. This, to me, is the golden rule.*
>
> *If anxiety or insecurity arises in my inner space, I honour it, recognizing that all is energy; anxiety, too, can exist. When action is needed in a situation, anxiety doesn't have to inhibit that action when you are on the ground floor; and, in fact, when you honour what you feel as energy, the frequency of it is often helpful in moment-to-moment interactions with others. For example, the other day I was driving and a dog ran in front of my car; there was no time to think about it; there was only enough time to act. Thought would not have been helpful, and the surge of adrenalin (the*

feeling) was a useful and appropriate energy in that situation.

When energy is seen as impersonal, it is also given the freedom to exist in the universe, and is not seen as being 'about me'. Who am I to make it go away, either in myself or another? Who am I to say that a person should not feel angry, upset, hurt, or sad? When you are comfortable feeling the various frequencies of energy and emotion in yourself, you automatically give the people you are with a space of freedom to be where they are and feel what they feel. You can test this out in yourself by asking the question, "Would I rather be honoured as I am? Or have someone try to change me?"

Practical application: Elevator down

This practice is a good one for visual people.

- Imagine that you are on the top floor of a building. (This is your thoughts about the situation, or your 'story' about it.)

- Visualize yourself getting onto an elevator. (The elevator is what you feel, whatever is up for you right now, sadness, hurt, anxiety, love, etc.)

- Take a moment to really get in touch with the feeling that's in your body, where is it? Drop yourself into the feeling as much as you can.

- Imagine that you are now hitting the 'down' button on the elevator (the 'down' button is taking you, floor by floor, deeper into the energy of the feeling. With each floor, you are also moving further and further away from the story, or your thoughts about the feelings)

- When you hit the ground floor, stay with the energy of the feeling with no story or thoughts attached to it.

Love in relationships

When everything is peeled back to raw frequency, the remaining quality is a very subtle feeling that I would call Love. This energy of Love, though, has a different quality than emotional love. We have talked about how the mind claims the frequencies (or fluctuations in consciousness) that arise in your inner space, and in relationships it is not any different. The people in your life are not separate from you, just like you are not separate from the reflection in the mirror.

The flip side of contained love is hatred. This essential Love is way too huge and slippery to be possessed. As soon as we try to possess Love, everything can seem as a threat to its security, and the whole thing can flip into hatred in an instant. The true nature of Love has no opposite and it cannot be contained; in recognizing the vastness of Love, its freedom will envelop you.

Claiming personal ownership of Love is like a fish trying to claim a piece of the water; no matter how much it seems like it might work, it never will. Like it or not, Love is always free. Once this is recognized within you, it is much easier to allow the people in your life the space to simply be who they are. When you feel intimately connected to the essence of Love—this Love with no opposite—you automatically stop seeking to find it in another. When you are not seeking to find Love, you can be truly available to the people who *are already* right before you.

Likewise, when you are willing to feel all frequencies as energy, you lose any reasons to avoid honouring people as they are. Being defenceless in relationships allows you to *meet* the people in your life from a place of openness and presence, rather than trying to fix or change them.

> *One thing I noticed in myself was a tendency to 'hyper teach' the people around me. When this quality was investigated, I discovered that it was a defence mechanism designed to make sure the person knew how to behave around me. When I looked a little closer I realized that I believed that if they behaved 'wrongly' around me, then I might get hurt. Once this unconscious belief was brought to light, I could consciously choose to not buy into it anymore. I could see in real time that I actually am OK. The frequency of 'hurt' is also an energy that I can allow, especially when I recognize that it doesn't belong to me. Hurt is a frequency that is universal and we all will feel it from time to time. While the story may be different, the frequency is the same. In being comfortable with the energy of 'hurt', I could then relax in my relationships, allowing the people around me to just to be as they are. Trying to educate a person, or fix them, is yet another defence mechanism; when you are comfortable with what is right here right now, then the people around you are given permission to simply be.*

Practical application: Partner meditation

This meditation can be done with two people or a single person. If you are alone right now, visualize that the person you are thinking of is with you. If the person is here with you now, then read the following out loud and practice it together.

- Close your eyes and allow yourself to relax for a moment.
- Bring to mind a person who you love or are close to.
- For a few moments inwardly give permission for this person to be exactly as they are.
- Intentionally give them space to feel what they feel, even if it is anger directed at you. Remember all is energy, and even if they are angry at you, that frequency does not belong to them, any more than it belongs to you.
- For a little while longer, BE with this person and simply honour them exactly as they are right now.
- Like Michelangelo's *David,* let all defences (theirs and yours) be chipped away so the masterpiece that is their essence can be revealed to you.

Chapter 6

Trauma and fear of loss

Another core aspect of 'the story of me' is the fear of loss and abandonment.

During my ongoing discovery of all that it means to grow, deepen, and mature in my humanity, I discovered a deep-seated fear. This fear was relentless. It was the fear of loss, and specifically the fear of losing love. After the sudden death of a dear friend, this realization moved front and center, and an opportunity to dive into what this fear was about presented itself. I knew that avoiding the feelings of loss and grief were no longer an option, and so I dove deeply into the feelings of pain, heartbreak, sorrow, and loss. This pain seemed never ending; I dove and dove, unwilling to hide from it or to shrink from it, I was determined to see what was at the bottom. After what seemed like an endless journey, I reached a place inside that I knew was beyond all time, all space, and prior to all form. It was a place of pure frequency; I was aligning to the frequency of original pain, the pain of separation.

In time I began to realize that by facing this fear of loss, by aligning with pain as a frequency, I was finally allowing it to really be felt and honoured. I realized how much beauty there was in honouring pain as it is, instead of trying to push it away. I could now give pain the freedom to exist as it is, and teach me its ancient knowledge.

This pain did indeed have a message of deep and ancient wisdom to share. Pain showed me how to hold sadness and grief like you would hold a beloved and precious child. This practice of holding pain, in Love, led me to develop the strength and courage needed to let Divine Love reach in to new layers and levels of the human heart. Like a cave of endless potential, my heart began to expand to levels I never before thought possible.

The core fear

The 'story of me' is usually built up around one big fear. This big fear is the very thing the 'story of me' is (seemingly) protecting us from. For me the big fear was some variation on being unloved, abandoned, or rejected. Aligning with a core fear as a frequency, and being willing to sit with it, dissolves the walls of protection because they are no longer needed.

Most of us don't have a core fear that is based on anything valid; usually the core fear is based on an idea that was formulated at a very young age. For example, if there is a fear in this moment about getting hit by a car, addressing the fear has nothing to do with literally standing out on the street in traffic. The idea is more about finding the unconscious fears that we started believing at a very early age. We can verify if this is a realistic human survival fear vs. a core fear of 'the story of me' with a simple test. Take time to really investigate the fear; if it comes from a place where the fear *does not make sense,* you know you are hitting on the core fear of your story.

For example, you might think, "My core fear is one of rejection and abandonment; if I am afraid in this moment that someone will reject me, does it actually and genuinely threaten my survival in any way? No, therefore it doesn't make sense. The truth is, in this moment I am safe, and no matter how big or looming that fear feels as energy, it cannot alter the truth of this moment." You can also take the investigation one step further and recognize that even though your safety would not be threatened in this moment if someone rejected you, a child's safety would. For a small child or an infant to be abandoned would likely mean death; the natural intelligence and instinct within a child knows that it cannot take care of itself alone. This is the way to verify that the fear is no longer valid; it was an old idea that may have been valid at one point but is no longer valid now. These ideas are held onto and believed and eventually become unconscious. Once it is unconscious, we do not know it is there, but it can still drive our behaviours in day-to-day situations.

Practical application: Discovering your core fear

Write down something you are afraid of. To get to your core fear, ask yourself, 'What is the worst thing about this that could happen?' or 'What would that mean about me?' Asking 'What is the worst thing that could happen?' over and over will keep peeling back the deeper and deeper levels of your story.

For example:

- 'I am afraid my boss will fire me'
- 'What is the worst thing that could happen?'
- 'I would have no money and end up homeless'
- 'What is the worst thing that could happen?'
- 'I would be all alone and starve'
- 'What is the worst thing about that for me?'
- 'Being alone'

Keep going until you feel like you have gotten as far as you can go. You should end up with one or two words like 'rejection', 'alone', 'pain', 'death', etc.

You will know when you have hit your core fear because it will feel like the worst thing that could ever happen. It may take a bit of digging because often this fear is buried deeply in the unconscious. The key is bringing these fears into the light of awareness where they can be seen directly for what they are. Just like when a child feels afraid at night in a dark room and the bedroom light brings comfort and reassurance, so, too, does the light of awareness shine truth on our darkest and most hidden places of unconsciousness. Once our old, outdated fears are brought to the light of awareness, they can be seen for what they are. As soon as we are conscious of them, they can be re-evaluated, and then we can begin to overcome limiting ideas based on past conditioning. When the fear is addressed and held in the presence of total consciousness, it can be seen clearly, and our present day situations can be addressed from the unconditioned mind which is here and now.

Love can never be lost

The way to uncover inner peace and happiness is simple: be willing to stand in total acceptance with this moment as it is. This sounds easy enough, but when unresolved traumas and fears remain, our inner protection mechanisms will constantly work as a defence in their attempt to keep us safe. As discussed in chapter 1, the two common things that keep us feeling separate from Love are *defences* and *seeking*. Feeling separate from Love or feeling incomplete leads to looking for Love in the world to help us feel whole again and satisfied. Seeking to find a way to 'get Love' from the world, and looking in a place where it cannot be found, leads to distress. Defending ourselves from fear of further pain, and seeking to find Love in the world are like wheels spinning without ever touching the ground. Defending and seeking are mechanisms that never take us anywhere. Love and happiness in a lasting and true sense cannot be found within our defences, and they cannot be found in another person or anywhere else. It is important to evaluate seeking and defending in an open and honest way, and see if they are genuinely working for you.

An analogy that describes seeking Love, or defending against its loss, is an image of the sun behind the clouds. Even though we may know the sun is there and we may experience it from time to time, on a cloudy day it cannot be seen because of the clouds. When inner peace and happiness seem to come and go in this way, we start to doubt where they actually are. Looking into the clouds will never show us the sun, but when the clouds are blown away, the light that was always there is revealed.

In this analogy, the clouds are our belief in separation, our protection and defence mechanisms, and the sun is our true nature of eternal consciousness and light that can never be harmed. Believing that Love is 'out there' and seeking to find it in another (so that we can be happy) is a vicious cycle, and it is a cycle that will never work in any permanent way. Sometimes those clouds can break in the presence of another person and we see the shining sun, if we then assume that the sun is *only* in that person, and not within our own self as well, we continue to feel lost and separate. Feeling separate from our own true nature is one of the many ways we end up suffering, feeling disconnected from life and incomplete.

When we fall in Love with another person and briefly see the sun shining through the clouds, we feel happy and content. Seeing our true nature of Love shine is a truly magical experience. A common misunderstanding is that the Love we feel for another when we 'fall in Love' has to do with that *person*, when really all that person is doing is reflecting back the Love inside us. On cloudy days when we feel that the Love is gone, it is easy to think that we can find it again in that certain person or we look for another person who might help to reveal that sunshine again. The beauty in transformation is that through our constant investigation of the clouds we begin to see *through* them to a stable and solid source of shining light that is permanent and reliable.

This frees us from the fear of losing Love and heals the memory of the past trauma of a lost loved one. When the sun is constantly shining from within, we experience directly for our self that *Love itself can never be lost.* Love, as pure energy or frequency, is constantly there as the core of our being. The more we investigate our fears and are willing to look through our defences, the more we understand that Love is within us, ever-present and 100% reliable.

The benefit that comes from investigating our defences and looking *through* the clouds to the perpetual shining sun inside is the reassurance of what you really are. Being unwavering in this simple understanding that *what you are cannot be harmed* automatically taps into your inherent qualities of courage and strength. Defences can unwind naturally and seeking Love 'out there' starts to spin itself out.

Dwelling on irrational fears leads to a desire to control the outcome of life's events, or to try and control other people. Energy is put into preventing pain and looking for certainty in life situations. We may cling to a person or try to make them change or be a certain way so that we can again see that sunshine. The more we hold onto this misunderstanding that Love can only be found in certain people, or under certain conditions, the more we stay lost in the clouds.

Another advantage to working with allowing is that the more aware and comfortable you are with what *you feel,* the more natural it becomes to automatically look inward (to the sun) for Love. Honouring what you feel, and allowing life to be as is, relaxes and opens a space for you to fall into the Love that is ever-present, the Love that you are.

Seeking for more

Rooting deeply in the truth of what you are brings about a level of safety and reassurance beyond words. This is a directly felt experience that over time melts defences naturally. Being defenceless in the world opens up a space inside that allows for a real and authentic availability for life, and ironically, it is in open defencelessness that genuine safety is felt. This inner state is so deeply satisfying that it is only natural to stop seeking happiness outside ourselves. This end of seeking doesn't happen overnight, but I found in my own process that the feeling of settling into this moment was so deeply and richly satisfying that I could start to honestly say, 'This moment is enough'.

> *I am not even sure if I can pinpoint when this happened, but at some point during the unfolding it hit me that this moment is enough, just as it is. A blanket of enough-ness fell down around me. A light went on that said, 'You can call off the search, this moment is enough, nothing else needs to be added*

to it, nothing at all.' I could see in that moment how much energy had been going into searching, reaching, and striving for more.

For a moment I saw thoughts in a different way; I saw all these ideas about lack and loss as something foreign, instead of something personal. I could see how thoughts were fluctuations in a field of consciousness (which was still and silent), and how this 'me' was attaching energy and attention to them, calling them 'my thoughts' and 'my ideas'. I saw that I didn't have to attach a personal story to them but could see them as they are: a fluctuation of energy that I really know nothing about. A mystery. In the mystery where nothing is known, everything is just what it is, beautiful and appreciated.

A feeling of contentment settled down, or IN, like a healing balm that had opened inside me and oozed throughout my being. From this settled-ness there was a freedom to really be here: to really BE present with what is, and to give that presence to this life, not from a need to get, but from the impulse to serve. If there is no lack, nothing missing, there comes a deep satisfaction that just rests. The fullness of that satisfaction expands, or so it seems, and spreads itself out into the world, not to accomplish any particular goal, but to Love for no reason, to embrace all with the Love that simply IS.

Practical application: Reset meditation

- Take some time to really stop, as if hitting a reset button, bringing everything back to zero.
- The zero energy is a 'pure potential' space, where anything is possible. For even just 30 seconds, fully stop, and let everything be as it is.
- In these 30 seconds, be here as if the past and the future have been totally erased.

This zero space is a way to open the mind and see beyond all limitation and to let something new be revealed to you, a new insight, or a new level of expansiveness. Can this moment be enough, simply as it is right now?

Chapter 7

The reflections and shadows on the glass

Being willing to sit in your own shadow is a huge service to humanity. The more willing we are to accept our own darkness, forgive it and love it anyway, the more capacity we have to be tolerant and accepting of others. This way we can be fully available to the people in our life and have compassion for the full spectrum of behaviours that stem from the shadow side of humanity.

Reflections on the glass

The reflections on the glass from the story 'It's Time' become a shadow image that we lose awareness of or forget about over time. The angels didn't know that what they were looking at was a reflection because they had forgotten about putting on the space suit in the first place. The problem with these reflections is that we do not know they are there. Our reflections or shadow images are the parts of our self that we cannot see clearly. The reflections in our lives are the aspects of ourselves that we are embarrassed about or ashamed of, that we simply don't want to look at. The reason I like to call them 'shadows' is because the term really reflects that we are talking about something that we don't notice or are not aware of. It is usually an aspect of our self that we have at one time repressed or rejected. The terms 'reflections' and 'shadows' are used interchangeably in this book.

When we reject parts of our self, it is like fragmenting ourselves into many pieces; over time we forget about the rejected parts and assume that they are no longer there. Being freely human means you are connected to the totality of life, in other words *you are everything*. The pieces of life that we see and don't like are usually our own shadows; likewise, the pieces of life that we see, long for, and feel apart from are also our shadows. Anything in life that you feel separate from in any way is most likely a shadow. Reintegration with your full humanity and merging with the totality of life is reuniting with the aspects of life that we resist, avoid or deny.

Transformation is the return to oneness from the illusion of separation. During the change that takes place inside us we begin to reunite or re-integrate with those aspects of our self that we once rejected. Being one with life, or 'whole', means that we have fully integrated all aspects of life and we simply can no longer see separation anywhere. In accepting all aspects of yourself, you automatically accept other people as they are. When you reject an aspect of yourself that you are unconscious of, or resistant to, you will also not like that aspect displayed in other people. When you embrace yourself as you are, you return to wholeness by accepting all of you. This is where radical self-acceptance, self-love and self-forgiveness come into the picture. Allowing yourself to 'be as you are' can go really deep; it can reunite you with wholeness, remove any remaining notions of separation, and take you to perfect peace.

Becoming freely human is about surrendering and accepting what is already true: you are a being of pure Love, whole and complete. The surrender is in being able to honestly say yes to your whole self, to willingly fall in love with yourself, and to forgive yourself for your shortcomings. In this way we can shine the light of awareness on the shadows. The benefit to embracing the shadows and shining awareness and acceptance on them is that shadows disappear in the light. When you have integrated something completely, you are not bothered by it anymore.

Integration of the shadow is like reclaiming the parts of us that we had rejected but that we *didn't know we were missing.* When it comes up for us to see, it is an opportunity to heal past trauma or reclaim that piece of our self that was hiding.

There is often an inner struggle as we transform and shed our defences, and work with acceptance of what is. Acceptance is very simple, but that doesn't mean it is always easy. The internal conflicts we face are often very challenging, but through cultivating courage and rooting in our inherent strength and essence we can work through these moments of challenge by being aware, and loving and accepting our self in each moment, through each breath.

How the shadow reveals itself

There are various ways the shadow can reveal itself and the most important thing to understand is that a shadow is not a 'bad' thing, any more than is the shadow attached to your body. These are often *universal and collective qualities* that we all have inside us. If we start to assume that the shadow is 'bad', it just becomes further repressed instead of looked at honestly and dealt with accordingly. Assuming that the shadow is something to be *gotten rid of* rather than *looked at* also puts us in the same boat; this can lead to more denial of the shadow because of the collective notion that we 'shouldn't' have one. There is a huge difference between hiding a shadow because of *avoidance* and a genuine willingness to get to the bottom of it by holding the light of awareness on it until it is *authentically seen through.*

Victim mentality

Part of the shadow is the notion of the 'victim'. When we are feeling separate and disconnected from life, we also feel disconnected from the people in our lives. The belief system of 'other' is a great place for the shadow to hang out unexamined. It is a very convincing story when someone's behaviour triggers us or seems to threaten our safety. The glue that holds the victim energy together and prevents it from dissipating is resentment. My own process led me to closely examine resentment one day, and my discovery was that resentment was yet another defence mechanism to try and predict and control the world around me.

> *Today an opportunity came up for me to sit with resentment; when a feeling of annoyance and anger came up, I sat with it and honoured it as energy. As the energy dissolved, I realized that resentment is about holding onto the anger to protect myself from some kind of uncertainty. I saw it as a subtle form of trying to control the outcome, though also seeing it was totally futile.*
>
> *I noticed that the resentment was actually a defence I was running as an unconscious program set up to 'prove' or 'know' what was going to come next. Holding on to the resentment meant I was holding a person in a mold, and then 'proving' or predicting how they were going to act or behave, especially towards me. The truth is, I have no idea how anything is ever going to shape up. I have no idea what's coming next, or how it is going to play out. Everything will always arrive in my life naturally, according to a beautiful intelligence. People will always just be and behave according to what/who they naturally are.*
>
> *Then I realized it would be OK to let go of the resentment. It is OK to not know what's next. As this realization sank in, I had a wonderful moment of spontaneous surrender. The more the surrender*

to life as it IS steeped and settled, the more things began to slow down; I relaxed into the experience and viewed each moment as if I were looking through a kaleidoscope of frequencies. Fear shifted into awe, and I settled into a space of not knowing.

It was like looking at snowflakes: everyone is different and yet the same. But there is no 'right mold', no one perfect snowflake. Every one is perfect in its uniqueness, a variation of the same design and essence, and there isn't a right or a wrong way for them to form. Everyone and everything is a unique expression of one consciousness.

As I came out of my meditation, something about it felt a little vulnerable, and for a moment I felt very raw and open. I can understand why it feels vulnerable to let resentment go, because it feels like it is going to leave me unprotected, but in allowing vulnerability to also be embraced, I realized that vulnerability is not a weakness, it is actually a strength. What I had seen as vulnerable and 'unsafe' was actually a space of open freedom and pure potential.

Somehow I had misunderstood that holding onto resentment would mean I could control the outcome, and that letting it go meant I had no idea what would happen next. Yet, with the resentment in place, I was not offering life a space of freedom to show me its full spectrum of possibilities. This protection wasn't really protecting me. It was offering

> *a false sense of security by trying to predict how people would behave. By letting the resentment go, I can now be surprised, I can let them show me who they are, knowing that a false sense of safety will never measure up to the essence that I am.*

Trusting in the indestructible nature of your essence makes it much easier to embrace the unknown, because you are no longer bound by the idea you can be harmed. Without the defence mechanisms playing out unconsciously, we are also free from the idea that we are disconnected from the people around us. As essence and energy, we are inherently connected to everything. Yet through the filters and buffers of our defences it seems we are cut off and separated from the people in our lives. This feeling of separation can very easily lead to the idea that people are scary, unpredictable, and out to harm us. If two people meet each other with their defences playing out strongly, it may very well seem like they are trying to harm each other, but when seen clearly, you can understand the defence is simply doing its job to keep us feeling protected. Once it is seen through and clearly understood that these defences do not work in any real way to protect us, and recognizing that the true nature of what we are is inherently safe, our defences can drop and we can meet the other person with a deeper respect and availability. When you can recognize that the threatening or abusive behaviour you are witnessing is a defence, you can see that underneath that, the person is just trying to find safety; in that moment you can then meet the person with a deeper appreciation, understanding, and compassion.

We all deserve this safety; on this level you can see that everyone is innocent. Everyone is truly doing the best they can, and simply trying to assert their right to feel safe, loved and happy. Defences always start out as well-meaning and innocent. But after a long time of holding on to them and misunderstanding them due to lack of investigation, they become shadows because there is no light of awareness shining on them. The victim mentality cannot survive focussed investigation. A natural law is that shadows live in darkness. Unconsciousness cannot survive in the light of conscious awareness, though this investigation needs to be truly honest. Trying to make a shadow go away because it is negative and you would rather not see it is not going to work. That is like trying to pretend your shadow isn't there when you are walking down the street. Pretending it isn't there because you believe it *shouldn't* be there is very different than honestly shining the light of awareness on it. If you still feel that someone has wronged you, it is the perfect opportunity to bring that shadow to the light of awareness. Are you willing and honest enough to really look at what you feel deep inside? Can you be willing to let resentment go and free fall into the unknown? Turn the light of awareness, honesty, self-acceptance, and Love on all your ideas and notions of being harmed, wronged, or mistreated, and see what happens.

Manipulating and fixing

Our shadow aspects are run by fear-based thoughts and ideas. The shadow is formed as a by-product of not being able to see clearly for a very long period of time. Again, to touch on the example of the space suit, when the glass is cloudy, the only things that can be seen are the reflections on the inside of the glass. After getting so used to that being the only view, you miss the real panorama of life playing out before you, unless the reflections can be *seen through.* For example, if there is a feeling of sadness happening inside and it is avoided for whatever reason, that sadness then becomes the reflection on the glass. If there is a person standing in front of you, you will then see them through that lens of sadness. The initial response may be to want to fix or change that person, because the sadness *inside you* is uncomfortable.

When the reflections are seen through and the full panorama of life is being witnessed as is, any emotion that arises will not inhibit clear vision. Likewise when emotions are not stopped from flowing freely; a wave of sadness can very quickly arise and subside without resistance because it is seen clearly as a natural rhythm of life and human expression. When there is a clear view, sadness can be seen as an energy of life, part of the panorama all around you; in seeing this clearly, you can let all of life flow freely like a cloud floating through the sky. Instead of being seen as a problem to be fixed, it is given space and respect just in the same way as everything else around you is given space and respect to exist as it is. Whether it is arising in the other person's experience or your own is no longer an issue, because seeing clearly means living harmoniously, interconnected with the full spectrum of life. Everything can simply be allowed to flow freely as the frequency that it is.

Trying to fix a person is as futile as trying to brush your hair in the reflection of a mirror, because what you are trying to fix is a reflection of your own unconscious. The best way to resolve unconsciousness is to bring it into conscious awareness. Awareness is like the light that we shine on a shadow: when the light is bright, the shadow is nowhere to be seen. So, too, with consciousness: the more we are willing to look deeply into ourselves with self-acceptance, the more we shine the light of awareness onto all the unseen shadows. Once the shadows are clearly seen, they lose their power to motivate us to act in fear, and disappear into the light of awareness. With awareness we are freed from darkness and unconsciousness and empowered to act, instead, from a place of presence and moment-to-moment *free conscious choice.*

This can also be applied to manipulating our environment or fixing the world. When we try to fix the world to avoid our own shadow, the results are not effective; again, it is like trying to brush your hair by touching the glass. Yet when we are seeing clearly and are free from the limitation of unconscious behaviour, it is only natural to fall into harmony with the life that is around you. In this way powerful change can take place effortlessly because *natural intelligence is more powerful than a shadow.* Saving the planet as an avoidance strategy or a defence mechanism will naturally shift into a moment-to-moment recognition, celebration, and appreciation of the natural beauty that is all around you. Respect for nature is only natural when you are living in harmony with life *as a piece of life itself.*

The reflections on the glass are often projections into the future, driven by unconscious fears from the past. Seeing clearly means to live and breathe in unison with the pulse of life. Being in this flow will often naturally lead one to actions of deep respectfulness towards the land around them, because the full panorama and interconnectedness of life is appreciated as a living, breathing life essence that is no different from your very own.

Self-acceptance, Love, and forgiveness

So what about the moments when I *do not* feel connected to life around me? One of my dear friends refers to these moments as 'JAFO' or 'Just Another Forgiveness Opportunity'. The moments when we are feeling disconnected from the environment around us, or from the people in our lives, the moments when we feel anything but in harmony with the panorama of life—those are the best moments to practice self Love, acceptance, and forgiveness. It is also important to recognize that each of us will experience internal changes in a unique way. You will always be you, your experiences will never look exactly like mine, or your teacher's, or your best friend's. Honouring yourself, your own process and your uniqueness is a very important part of the integration and seeing through all reflections. The moments of internal chaos, intensity, or disharmony are the moments to be tender with your self.

Freedom, failure, and forgiveness

> *I have been noticing lately how much freedom there is in failure. I have noticed that letting myself fail, and then being OK with or forgiving my shortcomings, is far easier than trying to avoid failure in the first place. Trying to avoid something feels fear-based and limiting, and makes everything contract. Letting things be as they are opens the space for more alive living.*
>
> *To me, this is the liberation—accepting myself and others exactly as they are. Letting someone else be as they are, even when they are attacking, treating someone unjustly, or criticizing, takes the judgment out of the equation, and lets me fall into the heart. When life is lived from the heart, there is an ease and a flow to each moment, even when difficult situations arise. When the difficult situations are seen without*

judgment or labels put on them from past experience, a sense of wonder and curiosity can emerge. Accepting things as they are lets difficult situations unfold as a mystery, and can then reveal potential nuggets of wisdom, new understandings and a deepening peace.

Reclaiming our whole self

The 'reflections on the glass' represent the unseen, hidden and forgotten places within us that we unconsciously reject or repress. When we learn to see these reflections for what they really are, they can be reclaimed, accepted, and loved. When we accept and love the reflections, they are brought to conscious awareness, *seen clearly*, and integrated. The integration aspect of transformation is where we come to see all the ways that we are holding our self separate from life. Just like in the story 'It's Time', once the angel was able to *see clearly,* she remembered her true nature; once she remembered her angelic self, it was also clear to her what the original purpose of the space suit was, and she was then able to merge with and absorb it.

In this analogy, the space suit can be seen as the personality or our uniqueness as a human being. It was the angel's original nature that was really being rejected during her struggle, because that is what had been forgotten. With human transformation, this is an essential aspect to understand. What we are reclaiming and integrating is the true nature of our self that has always been there, but was forgotten. We do not need to 'get rid of' our personality or our uniqueness; the key is in realizing that they are meant to be united, as part of the all-ness and the totality of what we really are.

Reflections show up on the glass when we are not clearly seeing or remembering our true nature. Once this confusion sets in, it seems as if the reflections are separate from us, and because we don't like them, we reject them. Once it is seen that everything is of the same essence, it becomes clear that there is nothing to reject; you are always reclaiming your original self (which was actually never *really* gone, it just seemed to be).

In real life, when you try to look at your nose, you can't see it, unless you look in a mirror. The reflections in the glass are the blind spots in our psyche, the aspects of our self that we have a hard time seeing. In the angel story, the angel was looking at the reflection of her own face, and because of the lack of clarity to see *through* that reflection she mistook the reflection for what was happening all around her. This example shows how when we lack the clarity and the certainty of our original nature, we see a reflection of our self superimposed on the other people in our life. Just like the angel in the story, we don't know this is what is happening, because we have forgotten what we are. By embracing the reflections that we see, we are always embracing our own self.

When a person in your life annoys or upsets you, they are revealing one of these hidden aspects to you, and this is your opportunity to see it clearly. When a person is acting in a way that triggers you, makes you irritated or upset, those are your golden moments to reclaim and integrate any aspect of your self that you may have been avoiding. This is the moment to reclaim your original nature, to choose to stop rejecting an idea of separateness and embrace what you really are. It is important to remember that no matter what the reflection appears to be, what you are reclaiming is always your original essence at the core. These are the moments when the unconscious is rising up to the surface to be seen through with the light of awareness. The key to seeing clearly is *willingness and self Love.* Being able to look closely at a shadow is not always easy, and it can even be wrapped in feelings of shame or guilt; this is where the willingness to forgive yourself and to love and accept yourself as you are comes in.

Integration: merging two into one

Things are not always as they appear; when we react from unconscious fears or past beliefs that are no longer valid, it is like being cemented into a fixed position, one that is inflexible and unmoving. When the light of awareness shines on these fixed positions or opinions, they can be seen for what they are. Just as with shining a light on a shadow, what remains is the truth of what was already there; the shadow was merely a reflection that was blocking our view. The benefit of looking very closely at our reflections is that when we investigate our personal reactions closely, we bring them into the light of awareness. The light of awareness can then reveal what was already there (and has never left), even when it was temporarily covered up by a fleeting emotional reaction or a fear-based idea. What you are as conscious eternal presence has always been here, the peace and happiness that comes with that realization is worth more than anything the world of forms can bring.

Practical application: Shadow meditation

This practice is best done when the feelings are fresh; save this meditation to use during times when something someone has said is bothering you, or you are feeling annoyed or offended by someone's actions.

- Take a moment to relax into the *feeling* that is present.
- Imagine that you are holding the feeling (as frequency) in the same way that you would hold a newborn baby.
- Surround the energy in Love and tenderness.
- Be curious, and willing to be shown how to look at the shadow with the light of awareness, through Love and acceptance.
- Notice what insights come to you as you sit still in the feeling; it is through facing and being with what we don't like that defences dissolve.

As we reclaim our shadows through self-acceptance, our defences melt. This brings us closer and closer to life; the more our walls of defensiveness fall away, the less we experience a sense of separation. This feeling of integration with all of life means that we cannot see any shadows or any separation from the flow of life here and now. The 'Divine' and the 'human' can now be experienced as equally valuable, equally spiritual, and equally part of the amazing displays of natural intelligence playing out moment to moment.

Reclaiming our whole self is really about embracing everything you discover about yourself in your journey through life, and accepting the light and the dark within yourself and loving yourself as you are. Self-Love and acceptance isn't just about cleaning out the unconscious 'closet' where the skeletons are hiding; it is about living with the closet doors always open. When the doors are open, the light shines in the closet, and the skeletons can be seen clearly. When they are seen clearly, we recognize they are not something to fear or avoid, but something else to love.

Feelings of inner conflict

When it is felt that the space suit (human personality) and the angelic nature (pure consciousness) are two separate and conflicting things, it is only natural to feel torn between them. There are certain qualities of the space suit that are designed to assist us in navigating the human experience, and are not meant to be extracted. In the story 'It's Time', the angel remembers her true nature, and shines her light *through* the space suit, absorbing it completely. The merging of the two is a very important aspect of transformation; as we reclaim those aspects of our self that we once rejected, the inner conflicts are reconciled and we can relax into our divinity as well as our own uniqueness. Going through a transformation, and realizing your true nature as pure Love or eternal consciousness doesn't mean you lose your personality. The personality is united with the totality of all.

A very common misunderstanding is that you have to get rid of aspects of yourself in order to be a spiritual person. This

Love Doesn't Mind.

Love is never offended
by your excuses ...
It is simple
like the sun,
shining ceaselessly.

Love is never touched
by your rejection ...

It is always
pure availability.

Love doesn't know
anything about your reasons
for hiding in the shadows ...

It just keeps on shining
every day.

Love doesn't care
when you pretend
it's not right here ...

It just waits for you
smiling tirelessly.

Love isn't bothered
by the hardening
you invent ...

It remains soft
and ready to flow
into any corner that's free.

Love doesn't mind
when you resist
its endless warmth …

It matches every 'but'
with a simple
'yes'.

Chapter 8

Living in the heart

"There is a light that shines beyond all things on earth, beyond the highest, the very highest heavens. This is the light that shines in your heart"
– Chandogya Upanishad

Deep acceptance of your whole self naturally leads to an opening of the heart. The walls of defence have melted, there is no longer a need for avoidance or denial, and so, there are no reasons left to close the heart. When the shadow aspects are not seen as something we need to protect our self from, the heart simply remains open and receptive for there is no longer a reason *not to.* In fact, the heart can remain open even in the face of heartbreak, loss, or death.

> *Several times in my own journey I was faced with heartbreak and loss. What I came to see was that living in the heart doesn't mean positive feelings and bliss all the time, it simply means being willing to feel and embrace whatever arises in life, through love. During one situation, I came to realize that the love itself remains, even when the form is no longer around.*
>
> *At a time in my journey when I was very committed to 'looking at my reflections', a dear friend died suddenly. I noticed that the old defences and avoidance patterns were not there to buffer the experience. (Not that they ever really worked in the first place, but I had relied on them, nonetheless.) This meant the heart remained open, and I saw that there was no longer a reason to resist the pain and feelings of sadness and grief. With the heart open and willing, I could be fully available to myself and my process of grief in a totally new way. There were no inner movements to hurry up and heal or to 'get past it'; each moment was simply there to be honoured as it showed up. Sometimes memories of him would flood in and my whole body would shake with sobs, and other times I felt his presence so palpably beside me that I simply knew with every certainty that nothing is ever lost. Each aspect of the grieving process was honoured with presence and love.*

> *I learned through this experience that the heart doesn't ever have to close, and the old defences are really not needed. The certainty in my own (and his) eternal nature gave me the freedom to embody both the celebration and mystery of a human bond and the full spectrum of feelings that go along with it.*

The phoenix doesn't rise from the ashes by running away from the fire; it gets burnt and then rises again. There is nothing to resist; underneath every trauma, loss, or difficult experience is a field of love rising up to be realized.

One of the most amazing benefits to living in the heart is that, through the openness and availability to life, amazing and synchronistic events start to unfold.

Synchronicity

Living as natural intelligence means you are aware of, and flow with, your inherent interconnectedness to all of life. It is only natural that synchronicities happen when we are living in harmony with our surroundings. The more clearly you can view the world around you, the more you will feel directed where to go and what to do. Being lost in projections, interpretations, and the rationalization of life gives us a very small view through which to look at the world. Much like the cloudy glass in the space suit, the angels forgot where they were and so could not know where to go or what to do. The parable points to our feeling of being lost in the mind and thoughts. When we have our focus and attention cycling around in the mind, rationalizing and analyzing what we 'should' be doing, there is a disconnect with the natural flow that is happening right in front of us here and now. It is easy to get stuck in doubting and fear-based thought patterns when we cannot clearly see what is in front of us. Merging with the space suit is like being united with the naturalness that surrounds us all the time. I would like to share another personal story that illustrates this shift from mind-based focus to living united with the natural flow and harmony of life.

> *For the last few years I have noticed moments when there is a heightened sense of 'being in the flow'; during these moments there is a deep connection with life. I feel a very clear inner direction, not from a place of making a plan but from a place of feeling inspired to act without knowing the 'why'. During these moments, inspiration is wavelike and clear; I often call them a 'download' to my friends, as the term best describes the feeling of lucid clarity and inspired thought that is rooted in the present moment. The sensation can be best described as being like a waterfall of energy rushing through my body. There is no notion of the inner direction being a means to an end, and it never occurs to me in those moments to stop and ask 'why?' or to gather proof. It is not because I am trying to remove those elements but simply because they are not thought of; it just doesn't occur to me to question that flow as it is coming in. Yet when I look back on the 'downloads', I can then question them, as if the rational part of the mind has turned back on. With the rational mind on, I can see that these downloads are a means to an end, purposeful in some way or other.*

It is difficult to put the space into words, other than to say there is no fear there. It is a space that is empty of fear, doubt, or the rational aspect of the mind. Fear can come in, however, once I start questioning things, thinking about them, analyzing them or second-guessing them. It is almost as if that state of consciousness vibrates differently than fear, (not that fear is unwelcome there, but that it simply cannot be found).

Over time, I have noticed the 'downloads' occurring more and more frequently and I can tell that this, too, is being integrated into my day-to-day human experience. At first they seemed different than the normal space of thinking, analyzing, and questioning so that I could really see the contrast when the 'download' would happen. They were so different, in fact, that for a while I thought I was channelling, or that the inspired thought was coming from somewhere outside myself. Now that they are happening so frequently, it is more like a feeling of just ordinary being, and this space has become natural. The unnatural way of being is the locked down or fixed mental position due to fear or the need for protection.

One day I was looking into getting some books published. I had been writing a yoga book, and had wanted to find a way to publish these writings so that my yoga students could have a way to practice at home. I searched for several different publishers and had no luck. One day when I was sitting in meditation I felt a 'download' start, the familiar wave of energy, inspired thought and clarity rushed through my system and the words 'start a blog' streamed into my mind. I knew it was an inner direction and felt immediately inspired to follow it. I got up and went to my computer and downloaded the free software. Over the next few months I published my yoga poses and ideas on the blog, and shared them with my students as well as on other social media. For the next three years I would write when inspired and post the entries to my blog. As my social media circle grew, I continued to feel inspired, and the inner direction continued to guide me to post my writing. I had no idea why, or to what end, and the notion of 'means to an end' never occurred to me.

Three years after starting my blog, I was contacted by my publisher and asked if I could write three books. I was surprised because I had completely let go of the idea of publishing any books and was quite happy simply sharing through the blog posts, but the inner direction came strongly through as 'Yes, say yes'. To this very day I have no idea why or to what end I am supposed to write, but I can look back on the moment of inner direction to start a blog and on the moment of the publisher contacting me, and see how trusting the inner directions and flow of life had orchestrated a series of synchronicities that I could never have planned with my mind.

The mind loves to complicate things; this is one of many reasons why it overlooks the obvious. When the mind is busy running its defending and avoiding programs, it doesn't take time to realize that in this moment it is actually safe. Because the defence programs are unconscious, they are running on auto-pilot, all the time, even when unnecessary.

The heart is content with what is here, knowing that if change needs to happen, it will. The heart sees that even the mechanism that complicates things is how it should be and, like everything else, has a right to exist. The heart is simple; it sees the mind for what it is and recognizes its important functions. If a moment does arise where protection really is needed, the heart trusts that, in the light of conscious awareness, everything will be handled appropriately.

Love will always embrace everything

Oneness with life, or living in the heart, also means that everything can be embraced and honoured through the light of moment-to-moment presence.

I once had a powerful insight that illustrated the power of the love, strength and resilience that is inherent in the Divinely-Human heart.

> *Yesterday I was having a conversation with a dear friend, and I shared my feelings of spiritual growth being like an expansion and then contraction, and how it felt like I was always taking two steps forward and three steps back. My friend's comment floored me: 'Yes, it is two steps forward and three steps back. The backward step is to pick up the human parts and bring them along.' 'Yes, that's it', I thought, 'that's totally it. This Love is too great to*

leave anything behind, or to leave anything out. It will always come back for even our deepest, darkest, and most hidden places of pain and fear; nothing could ever be left behind'.

It is through compassion that this Love reaches down into our deepest wounds, our deepest pain, in order to bring them forward and into the light of freedom. This maternal compassionate love will always go back for everyone and everything. Something in me came to rest in that moment, very deeply, and I began to see that this force of Love is not a two-way flow at all; it is a circle, one that flows always without a beginning or an end. Divine Love encompasses and includes everything, it cannot be restricted or contained; and Love freely given and freely received are actually one and the same.

Beyond all borders, all boundaries, and even beyond all planets, is a force of Love so powerful, so huge, that it cannot possibly be contained or owned. It cannot be limited or labelled in any way by any religion or belief system, it's simply too big for that. But most importantly, it has the power and the stamina to always go back, to find its way to any place, any depth, any level of darkness or pain, and return all its children to the formless arms of Love.

Service

Embracing your wholeness is the greatest gift you can give to others. Being sustained fully as you are, right now, leaves you empty of grasping at the world to fill yourself up. Being already full, you are free to just be yourself, as you are, moment to moment. When you don't need anything from the world, or from other people, everything you do is service.

Inner stillness and living in the flow

As the defences and reflections are *seen through* by the light of awareness, the motives for action in the world become very different. No longer driven by the need to protect our self from life and no longer seeking to become whole, the motive to 'do' simply fades. Personal goals shift to universal service, not as part of a new identity, but as an expression of natural intelligence to which you are intimately tied. Seeing that you are interwoven with the flow of life, you can't help but notice that *everything that is, is what you are,* and you cannot help *but* be moved to flow in harmony with that. Life, by its very nature, is a harmonious and intelligent flow. In other words, it is always supporting itself, and because you are a thread in that tapestry, you are perpetually supported by all of it in each and every moment.

Lazy Zen master story

An important distinction in opened-hearted living is the one between contentment and complacency. Being truly content with 'what is' means there is no inner momentum or driving force to 'get something' from the world, because there is longer a sense of lack. Feeling full, content, complete, and happy means the inner momentum to strive for 'more' stops. But this doesn't mean that action doesn't happen; it means that its motive has changed. Having no motive to fulfill a sense of lack means that you are available to life when action is needed, and content to sit and rest when it is not. In other words, when action is required, life *pulls it out of you.*

Once there were two Zen masters, who lived in a Zen monastery. When the two Zen masters realized their true nature, they became so happy that they started to become lazy. There were so content and fulfilled that they no longer wanted to do anything. Feeling so peaceful and happy, the Zen masters decided to leave the monastery and go back to living life in the world. They said their goodbyes and parted ways. After about a month's time the two friends decided to check in with each other. The one lazy master said to the other, 'What have you been up to?' and the other master answered, 'I have been sitting on my couch all day just watching the world in awe. I am too lazy to do anything'. The first master replied, 'Ah, I am feeling the same way: I am just so happy that I have no desire to do anything. I am sitting here just being content day after day'.

About a year passed and the two friends decided to check in with each other once again. The one lazy master said to the other, 'So what have you been up to these days?' The second master said, 'Well, actually I have opened a book store. and I am now the owner of a successful book store chain'. The first master replied, 'Wow! How did that happen? The last time we talked you were so lazy!' The second master said, 'Yes, I was sitting on the couch one day and the idea hit me to open a bookstore, and when the feeling of inspiration came over me, I was simply too lazy to resist it'.

This story is a wonderful illustration of how contentment with what is, in this moment, doesn't mean that action stops taking place. Living harmoniously is actually much easier and more efficient than the action that comes from an inner striving or need to be fulfilled. Being already fulfilled frees you to serve in ways that are inspired. In my own process, this shift from personal goals to universal service didn't happen overnight. For me it was a gradual change that took place over many years.

> *I keep wondering when the motive to 'do' something will come back, and it just doesn't. Yet life is still happening and playing out around me, and often through me, but I don't feel inside as if I am doing anything. Each moment I feel the sense of simple here-ness, and when life situations arise that need my attention, there is nothing inhibiting a conscious action.*
>
> *The feeling is one of being simply anchored in the moment; there is no longer a drive to achieve anything. The feeling of inner fullness and satisfaction is like a white noise constantly in the background. Sometimes it is louder, and sometimes it is quiet, but it's always there. Sometimes it feels almost like a beckoning to go and sit, and in those moments the white noise becomes so loud it feels like a complete absorption into the sound of silence. At other times it is quieter and subtler, detectable as a constant background noise even when there is movement and outward action.*
>
> *It feels a bit like running out of gas, but in a pleasant way. Since the gas has run out, I am simply resting with no movement; there is no driving force. But it is also clearly seen that, when there was plenty of*

gas and plenty of movement, the feeling was just a spinning of wheels with no contact to the ground. This feeling of stillness and lack of momentum is like a very pleasant sigh of relief.

And, interestingly, I have noticed that life continues to move and I am simply pulled along as part of that stream. When a client calls, or someone asks a question, the pull is there, and movement happens effortlessly and, ironically, much more productively, than when there was a lot of inner momentum.

There is a deep trust in the stream of life, as there is no sense of being separate from it. Life is pure intelligence, and its brilliance and flow is happening on such an enormous scale that the human mind cannot begin to fathom it. Yet the mind is intricately connected to it and equally valuable because it is made up of that very intelligence. I have come to realize that being free from my identification with thoughts and mental functions also releases the identification with time, past fears, and future fantasies. This freedom can then settle into the present moment experience of being a human being on a planet called Earth. Instead of being limited to, or bound by the human experience, there is the freedom to embody it completely.

Realizing that the field of consciousness is united, eternal, and liberated by its very nature, means that it can be celebrated freely through the human form and experienced through the eyes of a human being. From within the human form, we can realize directly the experience of consciousness being aware of itself, right down to our physical toes. Eternal consciousness and humanity are not two separate things; liberation doesn't mean you are free from the human experience; it is more like being *free to be human*, fully and completely.

Living from this simple here-ness and presence, we can meet life as it arises. Living in the heart is another way to say living in the now. This present moment awareness, and freedom from time-bound or fear-based thinking, gives us the freedom to be fully human. All it takes is a simple moment, one second, to stop and notice: What is happening right now? What is my present experience?

Practical application: Breath meditation

- The breath is always here and now. Notice how the breath can anchor you into this moment.
- Follow the breath to its source. Feel the aliveness within the breath, and just be right here.

Chapter 9

Divine timing and natural intelligence

I can understand flowers, grow them in my yard year after year, and I even have a PhD in botany, but there is no way I am able to germinate a seed, or burst open a bloom. The seed germinates by itself, and the flower blooms according to its own timing and intelligence. No amount of personal knowledge is able to do that. Nature wins every time. Sure we can influence its growth by putting it in the sun or in a greenhouse, but we can't actually do the growing, germinating, or blossoming; that happens by itself. From the spiralling of galaxies, to the sprouting of tiny seeds, nature is a whole and perfect mystery.

Natural intelligence

In my yoga classes I often guide people to rest and relax and find the inherent intelligence with which we are born. There is a natural intelligence that makes an infant's body move and breathe, an inherent wisdom that allows the baby to find its hands and feet and figure out how to roll over. Even though parents can offer a loving space of nurturing and support, it is something *within* the baby that allows these movements to happen. This is what I call *natural intelligence*; it is inherent within, and it is available to us constantly, guiding and navigating us through the human experience. I often hear people say that the human body should come with an instruction manual, and to that I say: it has one, but we've forgotten how to read it.

Again, it comes back to where we hold our attention, our focus. If our attention is preoccupied with the past or the future, or unconsciously running old protection programs, we are not able to hear the instructions our inner wisdom is giving us. This preoccupation also inhibits us from receiving the messages that the natural intelligence of life is giving to help us navigate the planet and live in harmony with other humans.

We are already connected to life and have never actually been separated from our natural intelligence, but because of our space suit, we don't directly experience a felt sense of oneness and harmony. The good news is that because our natural state has never left us, we can return to it at any time.

The pure essence of natural intelligence can never be wrapped up in words. Words can point to it, but ultimately the words need to be peeled back to reveal the language-less essence underneath.

Inner momentum and internal rest

I often refer to the sense of busyness and preoccupation with past and future as *inner momentum.* This momentum doesn't actually get us anywhere, just like a spinning bicycle wheel that's not in contact with the ground. There can be many types of busyness happening at the same time, such as defending one's self against people or situations; or seeking for a better, more fulfilling moment. All this internal activity turns inside like a spinning wheel but without actually accomplishing anything. Picture old outdated software programs running on a computer: as the program is running in the background, the computer functions more slowly, and the old programs are not even useful anymore. The defending programs are running based on fears from the past and the seeking programs are based on hopes for the future. Yet the only way we can truly move through life is to be pulled by the natural current of unfolding events that is happening right here and now. By learning how to relax our inner momentum, fully land in the present moment, and flow with the stream of life that is right here and now, your attention is free to hear and harmonize with the signs and signals life is giving you. Life is constantly supporting us, guiding and directing us in subtle ways, but when so many programs are running internally, we are too busy to be able to take their support.

Inner rest can be found in any moment by simply stopping and allowing this moment to *be as it is.* That way we can rest and coast on the natural stream of life that is designed to take us exactly where we are supposed to be. One great way to tell if there is inner momentum is to stop and ask, 'Is this moment enough? Can I allow this moment, myself, and everything else for this moment only to be as it is?' If the answer is no, there is a seeking program running, and if the answer is yes, that means that the seeking momentum has stopped, and so true satisfaction can be deeply met within you in this moment. For myself, I find it most helpful to not think of the stopping of seeking as a one-shot deal, but as a regular checking in to see what is playing out in the moment. By zeroing in on this moment only, you are dealing with what is alive and relevant. To think of it in terms of turning off the seeking function forever can feel like too much pressure and in turn invoke more defending functions. Simpler and more effective is to keep it light and take it down to one moment at a time, without attaching an overall meaning to it. Making our spiritual practice mean something about 'me' will further invoke the seeking function and place your self in a linear stream of cause and effect or a means to an end. Simply check frequently and honestly to see if the seeking program is running; it may oscillate between running and stopping, and over time if it isn't fed, it will simply run out of gas.

To check if there is a protection program running, stop right now and ask, 'Do I feel safe?' If the answer is no, there is a defence program running. The fact that an old program is running is not a bad thing; it is a great thing to discover, because by shining the light of awareness on it we can consciously choose from *this moment* in time if that program needs to be running or not. Making an empowered decision based on what is real in this moment is much more transforming than being stuck in an unconscious and outdated program we no longer need. Reaffirm often to yourself that in this moment 'I am safe'; this will shut off the gas to the program that is no longer needed, and give space and freedom to choose consciously here and now. If protection is ever really needed, you will have full access to natural intelligence, presence and wisdom to make moment-by-moment conscious choices.

I consider the transformation process as something natural, as natural as a caterpillar becoming a butterfly. In holding it lightly, it takes the pressure off and doesn't become part of the story about me, or another thing to 'do'. Life is already liberated, natural intelligence is already clear, wise and harmonious; to shift your focus from the personal story to *life itself* means that you naturally inherit all the Divine qualities life has to offer. Instead of being limited by the space suit, you see through it to the beautiful essence of life that is here. Trying to own the qualities of life and contain them in a story about a person will not help in dissolving the space suit.

At some point you have to just let go and trust the river of life. The current will take you to the same place whether you fight and flail against it, or rest and coast, enjoying the ride. Every situation in your life, whether perceived as good or bad, is a part of that current, conspiring to take you to where you are supposed to be.

Natural intelligence is at play in the world of form. Ask yourself, 'What are the qualities of natural intelligence?'

The impersonal nature or impersonal consciousness

We have looked at the human tendency to personalize or claim ownership of energies, people, emotions, our roles in life, and our belief systems. Taking things personally is an indication that an old pattern or idea is playing out, and you have the opportunity to see through it. This gives an opportunity for conscious choice to happen. At any time you can shift focus from the personal viewpoint to impersonal consciousness.

Impersonal consciousness is like viewing the world through the eyes of natural intelligence. A beautiful way to depict impersonal consciousness is to look at a fractal image rotating and expanding (feel free to search for expanding or rotating fractals on YouTube, and take a moment to watch them). Watching this image illustrates very clearly a higher universal momentum that is taking place, from the spiralling of galaxies or the birth of a star, to the opening of flower petals; all is moving and flowing in harmony with this spontaneous rhythm. I like to think of it as a Divine symphony, each individual consciousness as a frequency, a note in the song of life. By taking a step back and watching the flow of life in this way, the sense of individual importance or specialness fades, and a greater intelligence can be seen playing out. This intelligence is also not personal; *impersonal intelligence* is an important aspect to understand on the path to inner freedom. Natural intelligence isn't a person saying, 'Now I will open flower petals and make the sun shine'; it is happening by itself.

For example, if we were to look at the orbiting of a planet around a sun and watch it spin and rotate several times, it could seem that there is an inner will driving it and we could think, 'Wow, it is so masterful to be able to rotate perfectly each trip around the sun, how does it do that?' But once we understand the natural laws involved, we see that the planet is not willing anything to happen, the rotation is happening by itself. The rotation happens perfectly according to natural laws. These laws are not personal, and no one has to try and make it happen. Another way to describe it is to visualize the various gears of a wristwatch and how they interact; the whole watch operates with its many parts moving in a synchronized harmony with each other. The synchronized flow can also be seen when watching our planet orbit in synch with the moon, which moves in synch with the ocean, which flows in synch with the animals and plant life, and on and on down to every cell, atom, and particle within the human body. This is the viewpoint of impersonal consciousness, the recognition of a greater harmony, from which you are indivisible.

The uniqueness of the human experience is that we have access to this impersonal consciousness (which is liberated and therefore limitless), as well as the ability to experience that consciousness through the eyes of a personal or individual perspective. When we are confined to and blinded by the cloudy space suit, or identified and fixed in individual consciousness *only*, we tend to experience our humanity as a limitation rather than a gift. Through transformation we become free to shift our focus consciously; no longer locked down in one place, we can freely and consciously direct our attention from personal to impersonal viewpoints. In recognizing that natural intelligence is liberated and always connected to everything else, we can have the experience of being able to move from one viewpoint to the other without being locked in one position or identified only with the personal side. We can have the benefit of experiencing life as an individual person, as well as the freedom to experience life as pure consciousness. When the freedom of our natural beingness is realized, we are totally free to move from one viewpoint to the other without being locked into either one.

Intentionality

Once we are free from the confines of the space suit and able to *see clearly,* we are no longer bound by the human experience, and therefore able to experience our humanity freely. Recognizing that infinite and unified consciousness is not separate from our individual consciousness gives us the freedom to direct that unlimited force through the power of conscious choice. The power of intention can now be consciously directed and focussed intelligently in our individual lives.

An example is placing a flower in a greenhouse to boost its own inherent ability to grow; the greenhouse acts as a catalyst to nurture its growth and enhance its blossoming. Intention can operate like a greenhouse, as a catalyst for boosting, enhancing and co-operating with natural intelligence.

Conscious presence or ('being in the now')

When the light of conscious awareness is free to shine on unconsciousness, we are no longer bound by time. Unconscious fear-based behaviour and seeking behaviours are driven by traumas of the past or hopes for the future. When *unconsciousness is made conscious,* we stop swinging back and forth between past and future and we naturally settle down into the now This empowered way of being is a natural quality possessed by all humans, and all that it requires is the willingness to accept and embrace all of you.

Unconditionality

Natural intelligence is unconditional by nature; a great example of unconditionality is nourishment. Nourishment as energy is something we all see based on its results; we cannot see the actual force that nourishes plants and makes them grow, but we can see their growth and know that nourishment is there. The essence of nourishment is what makes the trees and flowers grow and blossom; we cannot see the growth of trees happen, but we can see the results. We can also understand that nourishment does not distinguish between branches, it simply nourishes all, it does what it does impartially. Natural intelligence likewise does not distinguish. It cannot separate out certain aspects of life to move through, and not move through others; it is unconditional by its very nature. Natural intelligence simply supports life harmoniously, continuously and effortlessly. It is uncompromising, ever-present, ceaseless, and unconditional.

Wisdom, compassion and clear seeing

There is a saying, that someone 'can't see the forest for the trees'. This depicts quite well the inner experience of having a cloudy space suit. When you cannot see the full picture it is easy to make assumptions, take things personally and become offended by someone's actions. A good description of this is to visualize a mosaic, when you zoom in close you can only see one or two pieces, it is hard to clearly see what you are looking at. When you pan back, you can see that those tiles make up a face, and zooming further back you can see that more tiles make up a body, and a community, and a planet and so on. Being able to get an expanded view of the bigger picture is clear seeing. By shifting your focus from personal to impersonal or *universal consciousness,* you automatically have a larger perspective from which to see the situation.

It is important to understand the distinction between compassion that unconditionally loves and acts in the world, and projecting on the world your own pain. Only you can know which is which; by shifting into the impersonal seeing first, you can get a clear view of the full situation, you can now 'see the forest for the trees'. Once you are seeing clearly from the perspective of impersonal consciousness, you can then ask, 'Is there anything inside me that is suffering?' or 'Is this situation highlighting my own wounds from childhood?' If so, deal with that first before acting in the present situation. If your own unresolved childhood pain is arising and it is not met with compassion and love turned fully towards your self, then that pain will be superimposed on the situation. When scanning yourself from the level of impersonal consciousness, it will not matter one way or the other if it is a personal wound or a universal wound to which you are connected; each wound will ultimately need to be cared for by you in the same way: *through Love.*

Clear seeing is what helps us know if we are being moved by compassion to act and serve in the world. When we read sad or horrific stories in the news, it can be like a magnetic 'pull to serve' somewhere in the community; but without being able to see clearly, effective conscious action will not work. Unconscious fear-based reaction doesn't have the light of conscious presence within it, and so it is rare for unconsciousness to actually activate an effective positive change. When we are conscious, present, and willing to stand in a bit of discomfort, the feeling of emotional upset can sometimes be the magnetic pull that gets us up and out the door to do something about it. The trick is in being able to assess your inner space honestly. Being proactive in the world can actually be another way to run from or escape our shadow, it is easy to get very busy saving the world as a diversion for *not facing* our own feelings of distress. This can be a very fine line, and again, only you can say. The practical application below can be used in these types of situations to cultivate *clear seeing, balanced with wisdom and compassion*; when practiced regularly it becomes more and more clear how to effectively deal with challenging world situations, as well as how to accept and see through our own shadow.

When the quality of natural intelligence called compassion is balanced with wisdom and clear seeing, then inner direction and intuition will also flow in the situation, showing us what to do. That way it is clear if what needs to be done is inner shadow work on our self or the collective, or an actual clear and conscious action in the world inspired by Love and compassion. When impersonal consciousness moves you through life with clarity, you will be inspired to help out in the situation if you are so called. Compassion will at times pull us into action, and at other times will simply be an energy that is turned inward to shine the light of love onto our own past wounds and hurts that have surfaced.

Practical application: Compassion vs. projection

- Take time to investigate your feeling of compassion towards the suffering of others on our planet.

- Notice if the feeling changes as you practice *panning back,* looking at the planet as if watching it from the moon.

- Pretend you were looking down on the Earth through the eyes of an alien visitor. Do you feel inspired to step in and act, or simply watch and observe? Do you notice a personal attachment anywhere? If so, allow that attachment to be there and continue panning back. Be gentle with yourself.

- Do you notice any residual hurt, resentment, or grievance? If so, hold yourself in Love and tenderness as you continue to pan further and further back. (There are no right or wrong answers in this experiment; you may get a completely different response each time you do it.)

- From your perspective of watching the planet from the moon (or farther back), do you feel any movement of love or a pull to serve? Zoom in a little closer and watch your inner response. Notice if you feel inspired or called to action, and make a few notes for yourself with any ideas that come to you.

You may find that your responses range from feeling and clearing emotions within you, to complete indifference, or simply watching the Earth as an impartial observer, to being fully inspired to an action that serves the planet as a whole; see if you can remove the element of judgment from this particular practice, and let whatever you notice be OK. Practice this experiment especially during times when a news story stirs up feelings within you, and watch the different range of responses or inspirations that come to you.

Discernment and judgment

What is the difference between judgment and discernment? I like to think of discernment as a way of looking at and meeting life situations with wisdom and clarity, and acting from a place of empowered conscious choice. Judgment, on the other hand, is a mechanism of labelling life situations as 'good' or 'bad' according to our personal preferences or aversions. When we are truly present to life we can act from conscious choice; when we are unconscious, our reactions are often blind, and motivated by feelings of fear or lack. Judgment can often be used as an unconscious defence mechanism. When we judge a situation as 'good' or 'bad' we can no longer see it clearly because we have locked the situation into a fixed position. In truth, the situation may have some bad aspects and some good aspects, but when it is locked into one position only, we can no longer see the bigger picture.

One of my favourite quotes is from William Shakespeare's Hamlet, "for there is nothing either good or bad, but thinking makes it so." Using the 'I don't know' practice is a great way to see beyond the mental labels of 'good' and 'bad'. When faced with a life situation that is challenging, stop for a moment and simply stop knowing if it is good or bad; pan back, and see it with fresh eyes. This doesn't mean to detach or dissociate in the sense of *escaping* from what you are experiencing; it is rather that, when we can be free of mental positions and defences, we are also free to see the bigger picture. When our energy is not tied up in seeking and defending, we can then land fully 'here' and be open to receiving life as it is. To see our lives from the perspective of 'not knowing' is like a fresh slate where true discernment can then be written.

Judgment as a defence can play out in life situations in many different variations. When used as an unconscious protection mechanism, judgment can be expressed (or projected) as doubt, cynicism, bitterness, or criticism of another's actions. To illustrate the distinction between healthy discernment and judgment, I will use an example of a snake oil salesman.

Imagine that someone is selling a 'cure all' product that claims to provide ultimate happiness and freedom. If the person he was trying to sell it to was feeling separate from their inherent happiness, they may want the product and purchase it blindly without any further investigation. The action to purchase the product would be motivated by an inner sense of lack, and 'seeking' to feel whole. After some time passes, the purchaser recognizes that the product didn't do what it was supposed to do and feels let down and possibly even bitter and resentful. Because this person was not in touch with the *origins* of the feelings of lack, the bitterness would then be projected onto the salesman as if he were *the cause.* This projection is the defence we use to not stop, and be with, what is really happening within. In this situation, judgment can come into play, and the purchaser may claim that the salesman is 'bad'. The purchaser might also be highly critical of the salesman's character. In reality, the lack of happiness was already the (unconscious) experience of the purchaser, and the salesman simply brought it to the surface so that it could be seen clearly.

But if the purchaser could stop, and 'not know' if the salesman is 'good' or 'bad', it would remove the label of judgment for long enough to see that the heart of the matter is feeling separate from happiness itself. Instead of projecting the feelings of bitterness onto the salesman, the purchaser can recognize the true source of happiness where it actually is. The salesman can then be seen as *neutral*, not someone who can give, or take away, happiness at all; and the purchaser can be *empowered* to act from a place of conscious choice.

To a person who doesn't feel separate from happiness, there is no defence or *reason to resist* honest investigation so that healthy discernment can be applied to the situation. A conscious choice can be made from a place of inner freedom. There is no pressure to buy the product out of a desperate *need* for it, and there is also no *resistance* to consider buying the product, or listening and intuiting the situation from a place of clarity, presence, and empowerment. That way, there is freedom to check and see if there is a genuine resonance with the product or the person. From here a healthy conscious choice can be *discerned* from a place of inner empowerment. Being locked in the position of unhealthy judgment, our actions are often motivated by unconscious feelings of lack. When we are whole, complete and empowered, we are free to discern wisely, and our actions stem from an intention of 'what is best overall?'

Discernment and wisdom are qualities of natural intelligence, and can be accessed and applied to life situations moment by moment. By noticing judgment or criticism either in yourself or another, it can be investigated consciously and openly, when there is no resistance to feeling what comes up. Using judgment as a defence mechanism to maintain separation is very different than applying healthy discernment and conscious choice to a life situation. Again, this is a subtle internal shift that comes naturally with being rooted in the certainty of our eternal nature. Being anchored in our eternal nature and interconnectedness with life, we have no experience of lack or a need to protect our self. This makes conscious choice and discernment fully available to us in each encounter.

The 'inner critic' is often a manifestation of the idea that 'there is something wrong here', or a belief in lack and separation. I find it highly valuable to sit with my own inner critic any time it makes an appearance, either in myself or in someone else. I often lovingly refer to the inner critic as the guardian of separation. The following meditation can be one of the most powerful ways to dissolve any remaining walls of separation, or to see through defences. With the defences investigated and seen through, if discernment is still needed it will be fully accessible, and also balanced with clear seeing, an open heart and wisdom.

Practical application: Innocence and the inner critic

This is a great exercise to try at moments when you feel highly critical of someone, or when you have been on the receiving end of someone else's criticism. Take a moment to replay the situation in your mind. As you are reviewing the situation, ask if you can interview the inner critic, see if you can find the role of the critic, either as a voice with yourself, or as a character outside of you. Ask the critic a few questions; first thank the critic for protecting you, and then ask:

- What is it you are really upset about?
- What are you looking for?
- What do you really want?
- What will satisfy you completely?

After you are finished, take some time to just rest and allow the heart to open. Innocence is your natural state of being. Allow yourself to rest in a safe and quiet space as innocence. When you are finished with your meditation, see if the situation can be addressed now from a new perspective.

Natural abundance

The natural quality of abundance is the freedom to take in and let go in every moment. This *freely in and out* flow is natural abundance. For example, the trees are taking in our carbon dioxide, and we are freely taking in their oxygen. This natural and effortless exchange is an example of true abundance. If the tree held onto the carbon dioxide and tried to 'keep' it, or get more of it, the whole flow would be thrown off. This is the beauty of natural intelligence: by claiming nothing and owning nothing, you are free to enjoy everything.

Living in harmony with life naturally takes care of misunderstandings, such as greed or over-indulgence. When you are resting deeply in your inherent *wholeness,* the full expression of abundance can be experienced without creating an imbalance of 'more than' or 'less than' within your life. Knowing that in each moment you have enough, and you *are enough*, means that you can freely give without holding back, and you can fully receive without clinging.

The best example I know of natural abundance came from my exchanges with wild dolphins. Swimming with dolphins is a profound experience as they so naturally receive love without holding or containing; and at the same time they give love freely without claiming or reserving. When the heart is open all the way, giving and receiving are one, and nothing restrains the flow. Because there is no longer an inside and an outside, there can be total trust that love will be forever free and eternally here.

> *Ever since childhood I have dreamed of swimming with dolphins. During my first retreat on the Big*

Island in Hawaii, I had the chance to snorkel near them in a local bay. Seeing wild dolphins up close was a lifelong dream fulfilled.

On my first day of snorkelling, the dolphins arrived; having been previously advised by a few friends, I'd been told not to approach the dolphins, but to simply continue snorkelling and 'mind your own business'. They are often curious about humans, will quite frequently swim over and check you out.

I was normally terrified of swimming in the ocean, and phobic of sharks, but on this day I felt completely safe, as if the dolphins were saying, 'It's OK, we will protect you'. At some point when I was swimming, I could hear the chirps and whistles under the water, and the feeling of safety and calm strengthened. I looked up and could see their fins off in the distance, and decided I was close enough. Not wanting to disturb their personal space, I just floated where I was, waiting. My friend had asked me to stay close by, as he wasn't a very strong swimmer, so I was keeping my eye on him. At some point we decided to float and meditate, in hopes that the dolphins would get curious and come over to see what we were doing. I started to enter a meditative state, and let my inner heart open, as if sending a message to the dolphins that I was happy to see them, and could almost immediately feel a deep love and joy come back to me.

About ten minutes passed, and I was starting to feel cold; I thought to myself, 'Maybe I will just swim back. I got to hear them, and feel their love; that is enough for me'. I was secretly wishing for a really close encounter, though.

When I looked up, I realized my friend had drifted off somewhere, and I could no longer see him. I had a moment of worry that he was in trouble, and I started to look all around to find him. I had the thought, 'How will I ever find him in this huge ocean?' Almost as soon as the feeling of distress arose, I heard a loud dolphin whistle; I looked down in the water and saw a dolphin right below me. Immediately my heart opened, and I felt a joy rush through my body like I had never experienced before. As it came to the surface for a breath, the dolphin moved right beside me, and looked me in the eye. For a moment the entire world stopped, everything became still and calm. It was as if he were telling me, 'It's OK, it will be all right, I am here'. Instinctively I followed the dolphin; it was moving very slowly, and I was surprised at how easily I could keep up with it.

After following for a while, I could hear more chirps and whistles in the distance, and before I knew it the dolphin I was following was joining up with an entire pod. I stopped swimming and just floated in one spot, watching them all circling under me. After a few minutes I looked up, and was happy to see my friend's head bobbing in the distance. Swimming over to him I noticed that he had made a few friends, and was alright. I was so relieved that I hadn't lost him to the vast expanse of the ocean, that I didn't even realize that the dolphin had led me to him. I had a moment of second-guessing, wondering if it was a happy coincidence or if that dolphin had really come to me because of my distress.

After some more time in the water and the wonderful experience of feeling this dolphin joy, I decided that I had had enough and wanted to head back to shore. My friend reassured me that he was OK now, and so I headed back on my own. After a few moments of swimming, I looked up to the shore and realized just how far out I was. Again, a moment of panic entered my inner space, and I thought, 'How am I ever going to make it back there?' As if on cue, I heard that now familiar sound of a dolphin whistle in my ears. I looked down into the water and just ahead, saw the dolphin that had led me earlier to the pod. I felt such deep gratitude and joy to see him, and felt my heart open wide. He was swimming towards me, face to face, and as he came close I saw his mouth open as he said something to me. This time, instead of hearing the sound with my ears, I felt the sound vibration resonate through my body. Almost instantly, I had a sense of renewed strength and stamina, and I felt I could easily make it back to shore. About thirty seconds later I realized that he had actually turned around and was now swimming right below me. It was as he was my own personal escort, as he stayed with me for several hundred meters. Once I felt really comfortable with my distance to the shore, I silently thanked him, and gave him an inner hug. He turned then and headed back. This was the first of many beautiful dolphin encounters, and many more were also shared by my friends.

After some time, I realized just how beautiful and touching the experience had been for me, not only in fulfilling a lifelong dream, but experiencing firsthand the simple and humble presence of such an amazing being. To see and feel the compassion and care of an entirely different species was very inspiring. What I took back with me was the realization that this love and compassion is always enough, in every moment. The dolphins own nothing, they are whole and complete just in and of themselves; having no possessions or sense of ownership, they simply exist in an inner freedom and peace that very few humans can relate to. I was deeply touched and inspired by this experience to realize the inner freedom of having nothing but the presence that you are. It was as if the dolphins wanted to teach me that: in truth, there is really nothing to own, and no possessions to acquire. To own something you would need a container to hold it in, and what really matters, what is all encompassing, has no walls, no limits, and no end. The presence that we are can never be held in one place as it is free-flowing like a dolphin, and rests in vast open space like the ocean. In this space of free-flowing openness there is an ease and a trust that makes it clear this moment is enough, just as it is.

Insight and imagination and inspiration

Being freely human means we can access our full potential to create in our lives. Divine-Humans are natural creators; through imagination, inspiration and insight we are capable of creating unlimited possibilities. When the quality of imagination is balanced with insight and inspiration, we are free to move ahead with a great deal more energy, and therefore are able to make positive changes in our lives, and for the planet as a whole.

Being connected to our inherent wisdom, we see that we cannot control the 'waves' or interfere with natural intelligence. But at the same time we are also connected with our inherent *inspiration* to surf the waves that are here; this gives the perfect balance with which to invoke positive and appropriate change. Instead of reacting out of fear, we can consciously choose where we put our focus. This works internally, in our moment-by-moment experience, as well as in our life situation. People often say to me, 'There is so much discord and chaos in our world right now, how could I possibly relax completely?' There is a lot of chaos in our world, and recognizing that is *clear seeing*; but to approach that chaos with fear or from unconscious thought patterns will not change anything. Just like the analogy in chapter 5, trying to make changes from the penthouse will not work as effectively as getting down to the ground floor and letting yourself be consciously pulled by life's *natural momentum* towards balance and harmony. On that level, appropriate action is natural. Trying to solve the problem from within unconscious mind patterns is like a spinning wheel that makes no contact with the ground; stopping and being in the moment means the wheel can touch down.

Seeing everything as beautiful, and feeling content to simply 'be', doesn't mean rolling over and doing nothing in the face of tragedy or crisis. When the mind is calm and clear, action happens more efficiently than when the mind is *un*clear. When you meet what is arising from a place of higher consciousness and presence, an appropriate and inspired action can take place. When imagination is balanced with insight and inspiration, creative solutions can flow freely and, often miraculously, do.

Creative solutions

Creative solutions arise naturally when our energy isn't tied up in seeking and defending. When we are not feeling fully connected with life, our attention is often contracted around the individual 'me'. An unconscious sense of lack motivates our actions and the bulk of our energy is tied up in 'getting' rather than in an impartial—yet harmonious— contribution to the collective. When we do feel whole, content and 'full', there is a subtle shift in outward action: because we are already complete, just as we are, the action stems from an inspiration to serve the totality, rather than from an unconscious motive for personal gain.

Our energy is now free to face situations head on and deal with them step by step, because there is no reason to resist life or avoid challenging feelings. When we feel separate, life can often be perceived as the enemy, and from that perspective it's automatic to want to shrink back from challenges. When we are rooted in our true nature as eternal consciousness, we no longer feel a sense of separateness from life. The inspiration that action stems from is a natural contribution to the 'whole', rather than one from a motive to fill a lack, which keeps us attached to an outcome that aligns with unconscious fear based (self preservation) ideas.

Once our intention is clear and we are rooted in our union with the totality, we can look to an infinite supply of inspiration. Inspiration flows easily when we are living in the heart, and springs up effortlessly out of our connection to natural intelligence. We can apply a creative solution to any life situation at any time. If there is a tricky situation arising in your life, and you are looking for inner guidance, use the practical application below to access your own supply of inspired solutions.

Practical application: Creative inspired solutions

- Take time to observe your current situation impersonally, as if watching it from the moon.
- See if you have a personal investment in the outcome, and see if you can 'pan back' and view the situation as if you were an alien observer.
- Do you feel a sense of need or lack that you are hoping this situation will fill? Take time to shift your focus to the essence within you that has no lack, and steep in that for a moment.
- Now affirm to yourself that you are going to stop all doing, and shift into allowing.
- Imagine that you are hitting a reset button, or going to zero, and when the 'doing' stops, rest in what remains.

- It may feel initially counter-intuitive, and there may be a continued sense of needing to 'do something'; affirm to yourself that for the sake of this application, you are going to completely stop all doing, on all levels, for just ten minutes.

- Notice what arises or comes to you out of the space of 'doing nothing'.

What happens when we stop all doing and simply rest in what remains is that the natural momentum of life can pick you up and carry you. *Mental movement* and motivations have a chance to stop, so that something bigger can come in and *inspire action* from a place of infinite strength. If nothing comes to you during the ten minutes of meditation, watch for an inspired thought later in your day. I often get inspirations when I am walking, driving, or waking up from sleep.

Chapter 10

Becoming freely human and further integration

Every master was at one time a student and will always remain a student to someone. A student is always becoming a master. A mother is always somebody's child, and a daughter has the potential of becoming a mother. A seed is always becoming a flower, and a flower is always making new seeds. Stop time for a moment, and see the beauty of what you are becoming. There is no hurry; the life that you see around you is already flowering into an endless garden of beauty.

At this point we can begin to see that transformation is about becoming more and more free, empowered and available to our selves as human beings. Rooted firmly in our eternal nature, connected intimately with our inherent intelligence, and free to embody our humanity fully, we can now move on to living life from a place of moment-to-moment awareness and presence. I meet many people who are either going through or have been through a spiritual awakening, and a question I am asked over and over is, 'Now what?' How is life lived after the space suit is seen through? This is where the integration aspect of transformation comes into play.

To use another analogy, think of a caterpillar in the process of becoming a butterfly. At some point in a caterpillar's life, the butterfly cells will activate and begin to multiply. The initial reaction of the caterpillar is to fight this process, and it sends out immune cells to combat the multiplying butterfly cells. When the caterpillar goes into a cocoon, the real work of its transformation takes place. During the cocoon stage, the butterfly cells continue to consume the caterpillar cells. When the transformation is complete, the butterfly emerges as a completely new and different creature than it started out.

Human transformation is not all that different, symbolically, at least. To touch again on the angel-human metaphor in 'It's Time', the 'light beings' want to have the experience of being human. Unable to exist in an atmosphere of density, they put on a space suit in order to weigh themselves down. The space suit can be compared to the cocoon. The light of awareness within the angel's natural being will begin to spark, multiply, and expand at some point during our lives. Even though there may be an initial fight to keep the space suit, eventually the light of awareness will consume the shadows and the space-suit will dissolve into light. The light being will emerge being totally fused and integrated with the human form. Instead of seeing human and Divine as separate things, we recognize that they are actually both part of the very same essence. With the light of awareness turned on, it shines on the space suit so intensely that the suit can no longer be seen as an inhibiting or cumbersome barrier to life. Being dissolved and transparent, it's no longer even noticed; this can be compared to the butterfly consuming the caterpillar cells until they are all gone. We become so integrated with our humanity that it is no longer seen as a barrier to our divinity; our humanity is recognized as equally Divine, and every aspect of our humanity can be embraced and embodied. This way the inherent qualities of natural intelligence are not separate from us at any moment, and we can be free to tap into our full potential to live as Divinely-Human.

Shedding the old, birthing the new

So, what exactly does this look like in practical terms? To put it simply, what we integrate or consume in the light of awareness is old, outdated, unconscious patterns of behaviour (the shadows and reflections on the glass). These reflections are the aspects of ourselves that we do not like or have rejected. Our unconscious patterns are programmed to protect us from feelings we don't like, and are buried in the unconscious so we don't know they are there. Once we start to awaken spiritually, we become more and more conscious by the day. Unconsciousness becomes conscious over time, and we start to see that the old ideas we had in the past are no longer working. The more we become conscious and present, the more we see through old concepts and ideas that were based on a thought system of fear and protection.

When we start upon a spiritual journey, we develop even more thought systems and ideas about the spiritual journey itself; very rarely does the actual process of spiritual awakening look the way we thought it would. I often refer to these ideas about the spiritual journey as a conceptual map. To illustrate this, imagine that you want to walk through a jungle in order to enjoy a beautiful waterfall. Someone hands you a map of how to get through the thick bush and find your way there, and you start out. After a few wrong turns, however, you realize that the map isn't as reliable as you'd thought, and so you try making your way without it. When you stop looking at the map, your attention is free to see what is around you. You realize that you are not as far from the waterfall as you had thought; in fact, you are practically standing right on it. Looking down at where your feet actually are in the moment, it becomes much easier to find your way; following the sounds and the *'felt sense'* of the water spray, you quickly make your way to the falls. Breathtakingly beautiful beyond your wildest imaginings, you stop in awe and drink it in.

After watching a while, you look down at the map in your hand. Realizing that the trail on the map is totally different than the path you took, you start to second guess yourself and wonder if you are actually at the right waterfall. Heading back, you look closely at the map and try to figure out where you are by following it, and you go deeper and deeper into the bush. Again you make a few wrong turns and realize the map isn't the same as the actual trail you are on, and you realize that it is much easier to find the waterfall by the sound of it, by looking down at the trail under your feet, and by following the feeling of the water spray nearby. This is an example of how we get attached to our conceptual map of spiritual awakening: we form an idea about what it will be like and try to use these ideas to lead us. The problem with this is that the ideas were not accurate in the first place and therefore will never work.

I often tell my clients to avoid comparing their process with mine, or with a saint or sage they've read about in a book. It is not to say we can't be inspired by other people, but it is also important to recognize that even though a role model can encourage us to embrace our inherent freedom, he or she is a unique masterpiece of creation, and so are you. To read a book about spirituality and then to start on a journey with a map is fine, but at some point the map needs to be dropped, and the path beneath your feet needs to be realized. That way we can stop in this moment, and emerge as we are in our Divine uniqueness, and accept *where we are now.* Instead of trying to force our self to become something different, we can unfold in our own way and embrace the unique gift that our awakening offers the world.

The art of letting go

Sometimes we hold onto ideas even when they no longer serve us. Visualize a coconut with a small hole in it just big enough for a monkey to get its hand inside and back out. The catch is that if you put a peanut inside of the coconut, the monkey would then grab the peanut and no longer be able to get its hand back out. As long as the monkey is holding the peanut, its hand is stuck in the coconut. If the monkey would let go of the peanut, its hand would be free.

I use this analogy to describe how when we get an idea or a mental picture and refuse to let it go, we feel stuck and uncomfortable. If we can see that what we are holding onto is just an idea, or something we *think* we want, we can bring the light of awareness to it and be free from the idea. One of the biggest challenges is spiritual seeking.

> *For me, I refused to let go of the notion that one day I would be free from pain forever. I had an idea, or a mental picture, of what I thought enlightenment looked like; in my version of it, pain would dissolve and never return. Because I wanted that to be the case and was unwilling to let that idea go, I often felt stuck, frustrated, and uncomfortable, especially when pain would arise. What I wasn't seeing was how the frustration of being stuck was creating more discomfort than the simple vibration of pain on a frequency level. When the idea was seen for what it was, awareness was able to shine right through it. Being free from the 'idea about pain' and the future projection of how I thought it should look, meant being more open to pain as energy when it did arise. This also gave an inner spaciousness to be open to life as it naturally is, without always needing to know what is coming next.*

Freedom is not being immune to the human experience; it simply means that you are not bound by it. In clearly seeing this distinction, it is much easier to be open to life as it arises naturally in each moment, without having to compare it to your mental picture of how you thought it would or should be.

An example of this is a person who is looking for a romantic partner, or to have a baby; in this case I would ask the person what it is they want from that scenario, what is the very best thing that could come out of it? They often say, to feel loved, accepted, and complete, or a certain level of intimacy. An important clarification here is that qualities like love, connectedness, intimacy, and unconditionality are Divine qualities that are already within each of us. The feeling of love or connectedness itself as a frequency is not the peanut to let go of; the peanut is the mental picture or idea of *how* those energies are going to *take form* in our lives. How and when the physical manifestation of these energies will show up for us is a mystery. The way they come is often unexpected, yet perfect for us in our particular uniqueness. You can verify this by looking back on your life to the greatest gifts that have come to you so far: were you expecting them? Could you have predicted the sequence of events that led up to them? And if you could have predicted it, would you have wanted to?

Uncertainty and the unknown

Part of what makes it hard to let go of our ideas is because the unknown seems scarier than the known. The pay-off for having a mental picture is that it gives the comfort of certainty. The catch is that this certainty is never real. Even when we are 100% certain that a situation will turn out the way we imagine, it never does completely. By acknowledging this, we can start to loosen our hold on the ideas we are clinging to. Look back over and make a note of how many of your significant life events happened according to plan. Can you find *any*? The only certainty is *un*certainty. Embracing uncertainty and becoming comfortable with the unknown aspects of life means we are available to whatever does come up for us moment by moment.

Our conceptual ideas may seem to be helpful, but they are rarely accurate. The benefit to letting go of expectations is that our energy is now free and available to be open to the gifts this present moment is offering.

Integrating linear time and non linear consciousness

In chapter 1, I used the analogy of the amusement park fence to describe being separated from where you want to be. I described the fantasies that form the ideas about what you think the park will be like. This is like having a conceptual understanding of the park without being in the park. A great way to illustrate conceptual understandings is to visualize bubbles floating around. These bubbles represent our ideas about what the park is like. There may be 'strategy' bubbles that have within them game plans about getting onto certain rides, or just 'imagining' bubbles trying to predict what the rides will be like. Let me give you a few examples of the types of idea bubbles we often carry within us:

'When I find the perfect relationship, I will be happy'.

'When I have a successful career, I will win the approval of my peers and feel admired and loved'.

'When I am financially secure, I will be able to rest and relax and enjoy life'.

The *end game* for each and every bubble out there is to be happy, to be at peace, to feel wholly complete and connected to life and love. Oneness with life satisfies every bubble by connecting us directly with the source: happiness and love itself. In the analogy of the amusement park, the park is ultimate Love, peace, or light. If a person is separated from it by a fence and they long to enter, they will begin to strategize and fantasize about how to gain entry, and what it will be like once they get inside. Think of those strategies and fantasies as bubbles floating around their head. Let's imagine the fence is finally open, and there is no longer a separation between you and ultimate Love. You are free to walk in the park and directly taste, touch and feel the happiness. Imagine, for the sake of this example, that the bubbles are carried into the park with you by a current of wind. You don't really need them anymore, because you now have what you have always wanted, you are not separate from the Love and peace. Yet these bubbles are still there, old strategies and fantasies are still playing out. Part of integration is the dissolving or the letting go of the remaining bubbles.

Let me use a more down-to-earth example. Let's say that the thing you always wanted was to feel whole, complete, and loved. Thinking you were separate from Love, you developed a notion that finding the perfect partner would bring you that love. After looking for the perfect partner for years and years, you feel defeated because you couldn't find one. Hanging onto this fantasy seems a good strategy, because you *believe* in the bubble, and that it will work. One day you have a realization that you are not separate from life, the gate swings open, and you see directly for yourself that peace and love have always been right here. Even though you are now tasting an eternal love and peace, there is still a feeling inside that says 'not enough'. Often it is revealed that the root of the residual feeling of 'not enough' is the old 'game plan' bubble, or an old idea being held onto even when it no longer serves its purpose. Even though you know now that you are not separate from love, and you can feel it and live it and access it in this moment, the old idea still plays inside you.

The integration work is where we start to see through and let go of old ideas about happiness. If I had a game plan that said, 'When I have the perfect career, I will win admiration and respect from my peers, and then I will be loved and happy', that strategy becomes an idea bubble. The end game will always be the same, and the old game plan to get there will never work. It is like trying to imagine what ice cream tastes like before you have ever tasted it; no matter how close your imagining may be, it is never going to be accurate. That is the reason why it can be hard to let the bubbles go—we hang onto them because we think they are still going to work

In my own process I noticed my bubbles many times over the years, and some were much bigger and thicker than others. Some—especially the ones connected to my writing—seemed to take longer to dissolve. Even though I had been resting in the 'end game' space for many years, the old picture I had about how inspiration works was still in play. As Divine timing would have it, that bubble dissipated at the time I sat down to write this book.

Practical application: End game meditation

- Stop right now and feel the breath, and let this moment be all there is.
- Now ask the question, 'Is this moment enough?' If you get the answer *yes*, then you have reached your end game, you are happy right here and right now. All old bubbles can be released. The old game plans are no longer relevant and you don't need them anymore.
- If the answer you get is *no*, then really investigate that. Why is this moment not enough, what else is there to do?
- Honour yourself and trust divine timing, but also look at your game plans and see if they are outdated; are they still going to work to bring you what you want? What is your end game?

For many years during my transformation process there was an element of 'back and forth' between an impersonal consciousness and a personal identity, as well as between a linear trajectory and a nonlinear space of pure being that was simply here and now. In the moments of clarity and simple 'here-ness', there was no sense of being bound by the past or trying to achieve a particular goal in the future. There was no memory or attachment to a 'story of me'; thoughts streamed in as inspired, clear and purposeful, and the whole world was seen as essence. Life was a flow of pure intelligence and love. I often tried to describe this space of being as watching mould grow on fast forward, as if everything were spiralling and spinning together in perfect harmony with everything else, as part of everything else. In this space there was no experience of separation from life, there was no sense of 'me' and 'it' but rather a harmonious flow of existence dancing together. Life was seen as benign, beautiful and a sacred mystery, there was no sense of knowing any answers or needing to know any answers, and there was a deep quality of trust in that great intelligence.

At other times there would be a sense of being 'back' in a limited personal identity. I noticed that, when attention turned back to the mind and become identified with the rationalizing or the analyzing function, it felt like being squeezed into a place that was much too small. When thought would arise, it lacked purpose and somehow got locked together with certain emotional energies that happened to be floating by. Soon there was a feeling of density and a spiralling deeper into an emotion of sadness, and then a pushing up against a resistance to be with that sadness. The linear mind would kick in with a plan to get rid of the emotion and get back to that wonderful space of oneness and peace. Thinking that the analyzing and rationalizing were the problem, I figured I should ignore them or somehow resist them further.

At some point there was a realization that the two things are not as separate as they seem. I realized that my resistance to the natural functioning within me was actually another defence. I learned to drop all resistances—even the resistance to resistance itself. I then noticed that when the defences were not in play, the rational mind could have its functioning and purpose as part of the masterpiece called human form, without it blocking the flow of life that is all around and free flowing in this very instant.

The natural intelligence plays through the mind and all the human functions; when all is seen clearly, it is simply natural intelligence at play in the world of form. When I recognized that the human being is an expression of that intelligence, I could integrate the two. Rather than trying to remove the human part of consciousness that I assumed was limiting, I simply let go of my resistance to it. The natural human functions remain as they are, and kick in when needed, governed by a natural intelligence. Life began to flow much more smoothly with that integration, and I found that even the 'downloads' I had been experiencing for the last 8 years began to fade. Not because they were 'gone', but because integration became so thorough that I could not separate the 'high' states of consciousness and clarity from the very basic and ordinary 'here-ness' of being human. The Divine and the Human were seen as equally valuable, equally spiritual, and equally part of the amazing display of life moment to moment.

Practical application: 'Prior to' meditation

- Take a life situation that has been troubling for you and hold it in your imagination. Visualize yourself, the people involved, as well as the events.

- Imagine that you are rewinding the event, as if watching a movie running backwards.

- In your mind's eye, continue to play the movie back further and further.

- Rewind the visualization until you have gone before you were even born, before Earth was born, before anything was.

- What do you feel?

- On a feeling level, allow everything to simply be.

- As you continue to notice thoughts, feelings and sensations, see if you can keep moving 'prior to' them. Honour and allow your experience to be unique each time you practice this meditation.

- At the end of your meditation return your awareness to the event that you started with, view the situation now with fresh eyes, as if meeting it for the first time.

Chapter 11

Emergence

"To live fully is to let go and die with each passing moment, and to be reborn in each new one."
– Jack Kornfield

Divinely-Human, the beginning

Conscious living is where the fun begins. Instead of our energy being exhausted by spinning out mental projections of the future or defences against past events, it can now be free to really move though life with openness and receptivity. We are free to face and be with each thing that arises in the inner space or outer. This inner freedom allows us to feel and embrace life as it is and to welcome what comes with the arms of love.

Being freely human means we can honour our self as we are right now, and honour the reflection of life as it arises. When we are too busy projecting into a future, or shrinking back because of fear or resistance, our life cannot be addressed with full presence. Spiritual work is not something that you *do*; it is simply being able to be 110% present to what arises and naturally comes to you. Everything else takes care of itself, and the only thing you need to know about your work is to resist nothing that comes your way. Embrace, honour, and love all of it. Nothing needs to be forced, manipulated, shaped or avoided. This way we are free to simply be with what is, from moment to moment.

Silence

Silence is what comes before all thought or form. Silence is prior to thought, it is the complete absence of any fluctuations. All thought and form comes out of silence. Because all thought and form is a fluctuation of that silent field, everything you see, think, or touch is a manifestation of silence. In this way, instead of sound being a distraction, or a hindrance to peaces, sounds can be followed back into silence.

This can be applied to both external noises, as well as internal noises like thoughts or sensations. Thoughts are simply fluctuations in consciousness. When it is seen that thoughts are not a big deal, and the mind is not a problem to be fixed, then our attention can be free to go wherever it is drawn according to natural intelligence. Attention does not need to be stuck in the mind, and the mind is not something to fight with; thoughts can come and go when seen for what they are, a manifestation of silence.

Practical application: Meditation on sound and silence

- Observe your thoughts as they arise, and allow them to be there without any judgment.
- Practise seeing them for what they *are*.
- As you allow the thoughts to be as they are, look closer at them, watch from where they arise, and to where they return.
- Don't resist the thoughts in any way, simply allow them completely, and watch them closely. Follow them back to their source; watch them closely as *fluctuating silence* and let them pull you back to where they came from.
- When there are no thoughts, rest in the silence and enjoy. When there are thoughts, let them be as they are, and let them pull you back to their source.

Alchemy

The ancient practice of alchemy was based on the magic of turning base metal into gold. While I am using the term here in a more energetic sense rather than a scientific or magic one, the principles of alchemy can also be used with emotional energy to bring about positive change in our lives. Alchemy is based upon the principle of the transmutation of energy. To touch again on integration, when a reflection is seen clearly with the light of conscious awareness, it disappears; it is literally seen through to the eternal stillness and love that is always underneath it, though the essence of the reflection or the Divine quality may linger once the shadow aspect has disappeared. While alchemy is the same basic principle as integration work, the idea is to take the 'shadow meditation' (chapter 7) one step further. Once the energy we rejected (the reflection in the glass) has been seen through and embraced, we can then take the residual energy as pure frequency and use it as a catalyst to act in the world and bring about positive change in our lives. I would like to illustrate this with the example of the frequency of anger:

> *When you honour life as it is, it opens a sacred space where the true nature of everything can be revealed. A good example of this is encountering anger during my process of working with shadow integration. I decided to sit with the anger, and honour it as I would a cherished friend. I bowed to her power and presence and told her to come and sit and be herself with me for a while. She appeared to me as a fire-breathing dragon demanding to be respected and listened to. I told her she was welcome here, and I honoured her, just as she was. She sat down, settled, and shape shifted into a magnificent mythical being of pure Divine strength.*
>
> *She told me that she had been trying to get my attention for a really long time, but I kept rejecting*

her. She told me that she had been getting more and more insistent lately because I needed her right now, and the more I rejected her, the more demanding she became, so that I would hear her message.

I told this beautiful being that I was listening now. She settled a little more, and said to me:

'The strength that I hold is a powerful force; it needs to be balanced with love, honouring and respect. This balanced Divine strength is the energy needed for us to embody compassion. The suffering on this planet is great, and compassion is not an easy thing to have. I am simply here to remind you, and to provide the strength you need to fulfill the role of compassion here. When we hold the suffering of others with love and openness, and embrace their pain with deep love, we are reminded that everything has the right to be at peace, and to rest in the arms of love. Embrace my strength; I am here to help you'.

I was astonished at the authority of her message and internally bowed at her feet; in doing so, I saw great wisdom in her presence.

This Divine teacher called Strength made it clear to me that the role of clear service and compassion is not personal. The space of the personal realm is simply too small to hold frequencies like Divine compassion and pure strength; they need to be free, not owned. She shared with me that the energy of compassion is a very pure love, but woven throughout

> *this love is an awareness of deep pain and suffering. She explained that it is possible to be impersonal and yet warm at the same time when you stay rooted in the vastness of the heart. When awareness of suffering meets this pure strength and anchors deeply in the open heart, there is simply nothing that cannot be endured. I began to realize through honouring this anger that things are not always as they appear. I had been quick to reject anger because of its fearsome appearance, not understanding that it was the rejection and resistance itself that was uncomfortable, not the pure energy of strength behind it.*

This is a time of great change on the planet, and through Love, compassion, and accepting the negative aspects of our species, these energies can be transmuted and cleared, becoming a catalyst for positive change. When the negative aspects of anger are seen through, and the residual energy is balanced with the light of awareness and moment-to-moment conscious choice, what we have left is the strength and courage to face the challenges here and now and do something about them. When we fear our shadow and are unwilling to face it and embrace it, we continue to turn a blind eye to the problems we face as a collective. The frequency of anger as pure energy can be used as a catalyst in a positive way to unify the planet and bring about positive change. Through self-acceptance, willingness, and Love, anything is possible.

Manifestation

Everything arises out of the field of silence, that field of formless potential prior to form. To put the indescribable into simple terms, the field of creation is prior to form, and all form arises out of this field as unique variations of the field itself. Any fluctuation of stillness then becomes a form such as thought, energy, emotion and frequency, which appear to solidify into the world we see. Through the process of transformation and the practice of meditation, we can peel everything back to the level of simple being or resting in the field of silent awareness. However, being able to rest in silent awareness does not mean you will magically be able to control the outcome of life's events.

From this vantage point, as pure potential, you can now rest in the field of silence and watch the creation or origin of thought. When you see how life naturally wants to take form organically, you can then cooperate with it or flow in harmony with it. Life is always supporting us to be the unique beings that we are, because you are a unique manifestation of Divine perfection already. Allowing the natural intelligence to play out according to its own perfect rhythm and flow is always far better than what the mind could dream up. Manifesting from the level of the mind or unconscious thought is never going to work, because the mind is operating on a time delay. Life arises out of the field of silence, which is prior to the mind. By the time we are aware of a new creation, from the mind or thought level, it is already the case, and the mind stakes a claim to it after the fact. Yet if we rest in the field of silence prior to thought and watch as thought arises, we can then cooperate with the natural harmony of life. By aligning with natural intelligence and allowing it to flow uninhibited, we become like a polished lens through which that intelligence can play out in human form. Trusting life's innate wisdom and working with it (rather than fighting it) is like surfing the waves. Allowing the waves to rise and fall as they will, according to *raw intelligence,* frees the energy of our intention to work in harmony with the wave as it is. Much like a hawk catching an air current and coasting on it, we as humans can cultivate that same skill in our lives and glide through life with ease and grace.

This is not to say that mistakes won't happen, or awkward or challenging life situations won't arise. Just like the surfer doesn't catch every wave perfectly every time, it takes practice, patience and skill, which can be fine tuned over time.

Unconscious thought and inspired thought

Unconscious thoughts work on a feedback system of thought and emotion looping together while we are unaware of it. When a difficult emotion arises and is resisted, attention moves up into the thoughts and the thoughts trigger more feelings, which are then resisted by looping back into the thoughts. Unconscious defence mechanisms have a hair trigger, and when a perceived threat enters the picture, an uncontrollable emotional reaction occurs. When the whole feedback loop is thoroughly investigated by bringing it to the light of conscious awareness, and the feelings are faced with willingness to accept and sit with them (as frequency), then the whole system falls apart. Being willing to sit with the emotion as pure energy breaks through the resistances, and shining the light of awareness on the unconscious emotional reactions brings clarity to yourself and the situation. Once you are present in the here and now, you can move forward in awareness and respond to the situation through conscious choice.

When thought is conscious and planned instead of unconscious and looping on a feedback system, the thoughts are no longer seen to be important. This makes room for inspired thought—or higher thought—to stream in, and instead of being stuck in a loop, it can stream in and flow out without getting caught. You can also be conscious about what to do with inspired thought; you are no longer bound by thought, but thought can be used consciously in the world of form.

We are taught to 'think it through' or 'think for yourself', but without being taught the difference between unconscious pre-programmed (or conditioned) thought and higher or inspired thought inherent to natural intelligence. Without knowing this important distinction, the tendency is to stay stuck in the pre-programmed thoughts, which will not help us move through our life situations. The state of the world illustrates that statements like 'think it through' need to be re-evaluated. To put clear, focussed, inspired and conscious thought into a situation from the 'ground level' is very different than to be running fear-based looping thoughts from the 'penthouse' level, and analyzing or worrying about our world situation which leads to no positive changes at all.

Understanding the principles of pure consciousness, intentionality and the freedom of choice (that we access through transformation) makes it then possible to truly think for one's self as a liberated individual. By recognizing the oneness of our true eternal nature, we can consciously live as a connected individual serving a unique role in a collective whole. This way we can act from a place of conscious thought, think of the planet and humanity as a whole, and serve the collective rather than being bound by our limited and looping thoughts.

Cultural conditioning and the unconditioned mind

The unconscious pre-programmed level of thought can also be referred to as cultural conditioning. This programming happens when we imbibe a set of rules and attach a personal meaning to them, and then carry that meaning wherever we go. For example if a group of girls are friends and talk every day at school, they become a mini tribe. The mini tribe is also connected to the larger tribe of their society. The media and advertising industries from the societal tribe send messages of influence to the young girls such as, 'If you buy these jeans you will be well liked and feel happy'. If all the girls in the 'mini tribe' collectively agree on the idea from the larger tribe, they now have to carry the weight of that meaning with them wherever they go. Whenever they see those particular jeans, they will react with a positive or negative charge according to the conditioning that they have agreed upon. If they acquire the jeans, they react positively, believing the jeans will bring them approval, acceptance and happiness; if they lose the jeans they will react negatively, believing that the source of their happiness has been lost.

To the unconditioned mind there is no personal meaning attached to a particular type of jeans: they are seen as neutral. This aspect of mind is light and clear, and can make conscious, present moment choices based on what is best for all. The conditioned mind is full of twists and turns, where each one represents a set of conditions that need to be 'met' before happiness can be attained. The maze is never ending, each wall simply leads to another wall, and each time one condition is met it sets up another series of walls based on keeping those conditions intact. For example: acquiring the jeans as the source of feeling happy means that the jeans need to be kept intact in order to maintain the happiness; if the jeans rip, a new set of walls are now in place around getting them repaired or replaced, and the maze simply continues. The only way out is to rise above the maze entirely and see that unconditional love and happiness is freely available in this moment *as it is*. True happiness does not require any conditions to be met before it can be received fully.

Neutrality and mental labelling

When looking at the world from the perspective of pure essence, it is clear that everything we see is a reflection of the one consciousness. When looking at the world from the angle of separateness, one can be easily fooled into thinking that things are 'bad' or 'good', based upon their surface appearance or our unconscious conditioning. For example, when we look into a mirror, our focus is usually on our face. Because of our cultural conditioning, we may look at our appearance and unconsciously label a wrinkle 'bad' and put our attention into 'fixing it'. If we have identified with the idea that 'wrinkles are bad', and then plugged our self worth into that notion, the wrinkle may invoke feelings of despair.

This is where the 'I don't know' practice can be applied. To shift our focus to the mirror instead of the face is like hitting a reset button. Moving our attention to pure consciousness, or the essence of what we are, temporarily releases the hold of our social conditioning so that we can see clearly and make a conscious present moment choice. To say 'I don't know' if a wrinkle is bad or good frees us from the unconscious cycle of our conditioning by removing the mental label and our own personal meaning of what a wrinkle is.

Imagine an alien coming to planet Earth for the first time. For the sake of this example, imagine this alien has an *unconditioned mind*, like an infant's. The alien has no idea if wrinkles are bad or good; wrinkles have no meaning to him whatsoever. Let's say that you walk over to the alien and start a conversation. You have just been looking in the mirror at your wrinkles and are feeling self conscious and insecure about them; you say 'I am sorry about all my wrinkles'. To which the alien would reply, 'What is a wrinkle?' The wrinkle to you is a symbol, that carries the weight of its personal meaning, but to the unconditioned mind, *the wrinkle is neutral*, has no personal meaning, and is weightless.

Meeting the alien is a perfect opportunity to bring the unconscious conditioning into the light of conscious awareness. Often we meet people from other 'mini tribes' who carry with them a different set of conditionings, and this can often be the source of disagreements and heated arguments. As long as we are holding tightly to our personal beliefs, we are stuck inside our mental labels and unable to see clearly. To 'hit the reset button' and see the situation from the perspective of the unconditioned mind means we are now present, aware and empowered to make a conscious choice. When the focus of our attention is locked inside a mental label we are a prisoner to someone else's idea of beauty. Instead of seeing the beauty in our individual uniqueness, we try to mold ourselves into the beauty industry's ideas of what beauty is. To approach the subject of beauty with an unconditioned mind means discarding that particular lens and seeing the full scope of what beauty can be. Once you have unhooked from the mental label, you are empowered to make a conscious choice about beauty from a space that honours the full panorama of creation.

Intimacy

To the unconditioned mind, intimacy is the most natural thing in the world.

The unconditioned mind is free of pre-programmed ideas about how a person 'should' be, so when the people in our lives are met from the space of the *unconditioned*, they can be a mystery each and every time we encounter them. When you look at someone in your life as though they are a total mystery, or a perfect stranger, then you can truly meet them afresh. From this space you can be very present and curious about the person, instead of meeting them from old unconscious defences or expectations of how they 'should' be. Without the buffers of old defence programs, the people in your life can emerge and be revealed as the unique beings of light they are. There is nothing more intimate than oneness and, through transformation, the awareness of being 'one with all' returns. When you see everything as an expression of your own essence, life becomes a benign mystery instead of something to fear or avoid. Meeting the world from the unconditioned mind is like meeting the mystery that you *are* and therefore being fully receptive to life as it arises, because you are always meeting another variation of your own self.

When this is applied to human relationships, the relationship itself is also given the space to transform. When the people in your life are met anew, they are wordlessly given permission to emerge as their own unique essence. This unspoken permission is the ultimate affection because it touches people at the core of who they really are. When a person is genuinely honoured exactly as they are, it gives space for their authentic self to shine freely. I think what most human beings are starving for is to be seen and appreciated for who they really are, on all levels. When we transform our self, we are free to allow the world around us to simply be as it is. When we are resting in this freedom, we offer a miracle to others as well, because in our freedom to accept what is, *as it is,* we also give other people the chance to be seen, accepted, and appreciated exactly as they are.

Human abilities

Once we have fully embraced our whole self, and are living freely as conscious, present, Divine-Human beings, we can start to really explore the full potential of what it means to be human.

Living on the defensive, due to unresolved fear, holds us back from stepping into what we are fully capable of. Likewise, seeking to be 'something else' keeps us apart from the unique and perfect being we are right now. With our energy tied up in protection, defensiveness and seeking, it's really hard to embrace the full human opportunity. So far in this book, we have discussed the fear of past trauma and the fear of being emotionally hurt, and even the fear of death; but another expression of fear that can often surface during transformation is the fear of our own potential power and greatness.

Letting yourself be as you are, honouring your uniqueness and embracing your Divine-Humanity also means being willing to dive into the unknown. As we let ourselves go into the newness of this moment, and learn to embrace our full humanity, we may be surprised at what is possible.

Once we are free from the limitations of the past and the containment of future 'shoulds' we are free to be fully here, and embrace the full array of human skills available to us. Each human being has a unique and distinctive blend of abilities. A wonderful analogy to describe uniqueness is snowflakes: each one is different and special, and yet even though no two snowflakes are alike, every one of them is made of snow. In the same way, at the level of *essence* we are all the same consciousness which cannot be separated, but the way that consciousness is expressed through each human being (like each snowflake) is unique.

I feel we have barely scratched the surface of what the human mind and body are capable of. Throughout human history we have seen limitations and barriers broken down by the strength of one person's intention. The four-minute mile is a perfect example. This limitation had been set and then was accepted collectively, and when one man broke through that barrier by running a four-minute mile, many others followed. There are many latent abilities within the human experience we have yet to discover, and like the four-minute mile, as people begin to recognize and embrace them, they will no longer be seen as out of reach.

Abilities like telepathy are often seen as out of reach, or brushed aside as fantasies, or explained away as an overactive imagination. Yet we can watch a child cry about another child getting hurt or an elderly couple finishing each others' sentences after thirty years of marriage and not think of it as strange. From there it is not that far of a stretch to imagine humans being capable of higher and finer levels of sensitivity to each other.

My personal feeling is that spontaneous healing, empathic abilities, telepathy and even remote viewing are actually very natural skills that anyone can develop or enhance. If these abilities were seen as normal, there would be no hesitation to nurture a child who shows signs of deep intuition and help that child to develop it as a skill that can be used to serve the collective human family. Just as if a child shows a strong tendency towards music, we nurture that talent by giving them lessons. Abilities like empathy or telepathy are no different than any other human talent, and could even be compared to learning to read, play the violin or ride a bike.

There is so much freedom in simply honouring people exactly as they are, and encouraging them to be all that they can be. As we move forward and evolve as a human family, we naturally learn and develop more and more skills and abilities. The more we transform collectively, the less we will be held back by fear-based limitations.

> *At some point during my transformation process, I became aware that I had become very sensitive to what other people around me were feeling. I had come across a lot of different definitions of heightened sensitivity and became very curious and intrigued by what was happening to me. Through my research, I learned the term 'empath' and had a huge revelation in realizing that 'I am' an empath. This gave me the space and time to embrace and cultivate that experience in a way that could be*

helpful to others. Part of that was learning when and what to say to people who were feeling intensely, and how to 'hold the feeling with them'. I made plenty of mistakes along the way, and often pushed people too far and had to learn how to 'pull back' and give people space to work through their own energy and emotions. Eventually I learned how to move in respectfully and share the load with them; I started to learn how to balance being not supportive enough with being too invasive. I saw it like two people sharing a load equally and knew that all these feelings, no matter how heavy, will pass.

As I was learning to refine and deepen this skill I called empathy, I started to develop a fear of the responsibility. I became afraid others would be threatened by me, or worse, see me as special and place me on a pedestal. The one thing I have seen with pedestals is that we all have our flaws and shortcomings; to try and maintain a 'better than you' image will never work. We all have our gifts, and we all have our flaws, and somewhere along the way it all balances out. What goes up must come down, and to be placed on a pedestal always invokes separation, not equality.

Initially my solution to this 'problem' was to just 'be humble' (or what I thought was humble at the time) and to pretend I didn't feel what I felt (when in reality I did). One day it hit me, that my idea of humility was actually just dishonesty, and had nothing to do with true humility. I was simply draping my fear in a costume of 'humble' as a way to avoid the deeper truth. I realized that it is much more humble to simply accept the uniqueness that I embody and step fully (and honestly) into that as it is. Rather than trying to avoid my fears, I realized it was much easier and more freeing to embrace my shortcomings, as well as my gifts and unique talents: to be honest about what I am good at, and yet willing to continue learning in the areas where I fall short.

A little while later during my process, I realized I had 'identified with my role' as an empath and needed to let it go. Through my phase of learning to refine it, I had become attached to it and was therefore limiting it by calling it 'mine'. This turned out to be a very important discovery.

One day I was meditating with the 'I don't know' practice and I saw that empathy is something that simply goes in and out and through me, as part of me sometimes, and not part of me other times, and soon everything became too loose to define me in any way. Empathy was no longer 'my' ability, but just another aspect of the human experience that I can consciously choose to embrace or let go of at any given moment.

Eventually I made a choice to embrace the role of 'empath' but without identifying with it or being defined by it. At this point it feels as if it is just part of me in a way that is integrated and normal within the human experience. I also realized that the gift of allowing and embracing empathy as an aspect of my humanity, gives permission for other people to come forward and understand how to deal with empathy in a healthy way.

Embracing it without personalizing means that it is just another aspect of the human experience, not greater than or less than any other. Each one of us is special, and each human being has something of value to offer. A museum has a vast variety of creative expressions, and part of the enjoyment of being there is that everywhere you look there is something unique to observe and appreciate.

Some people are great at the piano, some people can write an amazing mystery novel, and others are extra sensitive to the pain (and joy) of others. In moving into a level of deeper acceptance of being exactly as I am, I can also hold the space for others to be exactly as they are. The message that comes back to me over and over is, "You are perfect, just as you are."

Practical application: Deep integration meditation

Ponder these questions for about 30 minutes; these questions are not necessarily meant to be answered, but more to loosen any fixed mental positions and opinions so as to inspire a curiosity and expanded consciousness. These questions often highlight where we are hanging onto bubbles, old game plans, or social conditioning. This meditation is intended to inspire you to see through the old ideas and to invoke a space of freedom and clarity. This free space of awareness also inspires new and creative solutions to what is happening in your life right now. Sit with each question and really take it in as a possibility.

- What if there were no fixed answers, no absolute formulas or solutions at all?
- What if there never was anything to be attained or solved?
- What if all life, all people, and all beings everywhere were given permission to simply be exactly as they are, and all that they are, right now?
- What if uncertainty wasn't a problem, and there were no reasons to predict what is going to happen the next moment, let alone the next day, month, or year?

- What if each and every variation of life, even in its seeming imperfection, is a whole and perfect miracle just as it is?
- What if every pattern of colour, shadow and light were like a single brushstroke on the masterpiece of life? When seen from the totality, would we really want to remove all the shadows?

Practical application: You are pure potential (*a continuation*)

- To be free from past ideas and limitations invokes the freedom in the present to decide where and on what we want to place our attention.
- Trust your intuition in this moment. Now that you feel content with what IS, and are free to be here exactly as you are, where does your attention naturally move to? You may want to simply continue holding your attention freely in open space, or you may direct your attention to a particular energy that is very tangible and productive in your life.

- In this moment you can remain open and free in a space of pure potential, but you are also free to embody something specific; it is all in the space of freedom. You can choose to embody peace or harmony, perhaps send blessings or light to a friend, or sit and steep in a vibration of love.

Being with what is

The more we have become free from our past restrictions, belief systems, and limiting ideas, the more we can embrace the full potential of what it means to be human. No longer held back from the past, or driven by a hope of future fulfillment, we are free to *be fully here* and embrace the natural gifts that come with a human body.

Being no longer bound by the human experience means that we can now freely explore: *what does it actually mean to be human?* Being anchored in the present moment and free to allow life to flow as it naturally *is* means we are free to embrace our humanity and all it has to offer. This is the point where we really begin to understand what it means to be freely human. You are now free to be fully human in all its potential to create, to express, and share with others without fear of being hurt or rejected. Free to fully embrace the gifts that come with the human experience, but at the same time no longer bound by its impermanence.

Living beyond the space suit is a beginning, not an end; it is the beginning of your life as a fully *free human.* No longer identified with or bound by limiting ideas from the past, as well by future desires, life can now be taken in moment by moment. No longer restricted by fears or resistance to feeling the full spectrum of human emotion, each moment of life can be allowed and received. Each moment is a simultaneous give and take; we are free to live in harmony with life instead of shrinking back from it or trying to fix it. We can live along side of it, not as a separate entity helpless to its effects, but as a being of light woven into the fabric of creation, in harmony with life as a free human being, and united with life as limitless and eternal consciousness.

Freely human

Freedom doesn't make you immune to the human experience; it just means you are not identified with it anymore. Being unidentified with the human experience means you can completely embrace all that comes along with being 'an earthling' and be totally available to life as it is.

Merging with life is like eternally falling into the heart of existence and seeing it expressed perfectly in the infinite variety of creation. The heart of my life is the same as the heart—or essence—of all creation. The more deeply we merge with life, the less frightening it becomes, because life is seen to be an extension of our own heart. What was once seen as dangerous is now seen as a reflection of the one eternal nature that cannot be harmed.

> *At one point I was faced with the paralyzing fear of ceasing to exist. This fear gripped me deeply and would not let go; for about a week, I curled up in bed attempting to fight off the feelings that were*

bubbling up inside me. I felt like a dark wave of nothingness was coming to get me, and there was nothing I could do to get away. I found myself in 'check mate'; no matter where I turned the wave had me; there was nowhere left to hide. I felt like my hands had been holding tight to the steering wheel of life, fighting to own the last remnants of control, to be the manager of my life, and my grip was starting to loosen. Inside, there was a feeling of defeat, not a depression but more like a sense of no choice left but to surrender it all.

I was lying in bed, fighting with life and fighting off the reality that I might not know who or what I was, when it hit me: 'What if it's OK to not know who I am?' 'What if it is really OK to not exist at all?' I realized that on some level I was dying, and there was nowhere to go but into the final acceptance of that reality. 'I am going to die, and there is nothing I can do' I started to feel as if the floor was falling out from under me, a vacuum of nothingness started to rise up and pull me in. The vacuum of nothingness swept through me more and more until eventually there was nothing left but a total acceptance of what was happening. Words cannot come close to expressing what came next, but for the sake of continuing this journal, I will try.

All was dark and quiet, even the word silence doesn't touch how quiet it became. Even to say that it was 'nothing' doesn't express how absent of existence it was. The fear vanished instantly, as if eaten by the vacuum of silence and stillness. At some point three words rose up out of this deep silence and remained in place, as if reverberating through a cloud of emptiness, 'one without two', echoed and lingered for a while, and then those words also fell away. After that it was just pure absence of existence, and yet, a perfect acceptance of what is, because this place was also the absence of all resistance. I can't tell you how long this black hole of vacuuming silence lasted because all sense of time and its measurement had lost meaning. But at some point an awareness returned of the room around me. As I got up and felt my body, I noticed that everything had a sort of glow, or a shimmering radiance, like an echo from the place I had just been.

For several weeks, I lost the desire to speak and felt very quiet. As time continued to pass, I started to find my voice again but continued to feel a sense of an internal 'hush.' One thing became very noticeable, and that was that life was no longer threatening. I remember one day being with a group of people and seeing them as if they were a herd of deer. They all seemed so harmless and simple; like wild yet benign animals. Over time everything continued to soften, and is still continuing to soften to this day. What was once seen as threatening was simply the essence of 'one without two' into which I had fallen. Even now as I close my eyes, I still feel like I am falling ever more deeply into a vacuum of quiet stillness, falling more deeply into the heart of all.

Within this realization of harmlessness and ultimate safety I recognized that life, and all its expressions, can always be embraced freely. Each and every expression of the one is deeply known to be precious, fleeting, and unique. There is not even a shadow of doubt within me now that the human experience, the Earth, and all its inhabitants, are sacred and perfect expressions of Divinity.

What I am left with at this phase of my ongoing journey are these words:

'Everyone and everything we see is an expression of timeless Love. Everyone and everything that is, is in the right place, always, even when it doesn't seem to be. And above all else; everyone and everything in existence is loved beyond measure. Nothing is ever excluded from this Love because there is no 'outside' of the oneness we are all part of; we are all perfectly inseparable from Love.'

Practical application: Living as Love

Recognize for a moment that there is no 'outside' for anything to be extracted to and therefore all can be allowed, honoured, and embraced fully and freely.

- Let yourself fall into your heart centre and intend that this is a sacred space. Imagine that the space in the heart is unlimited in its potential for transformation and freedom.

- Imagine that a portal is opening into a realm of pure, unconditional, timeless Love. This realm of pure Love can be found at any time in the heart, but reaches also beyond all dimensions of time and space, unimaginably vast in its presence and potential.

- Allow yourself to fall into this space with total acceptance, knowing that you are safe, loved, and held. Intend that you are falling into a cocoon of timeless Love, and limitless potential for transformation.

- Mentally affirm, 'I am that, I am Love, I am', over and over until you feel ready to simply fall into the essence of love itself.

- Let this feeling of Love and acceptance travel to your physical body, from the cells into the molecules atoms and particles and all the way to the very depths of your being; so that everything in you now vibrates to this frequency of Love.

- Take a few more moments to align the vibration of the physical body to the frequency of Love.

Living in the heart

Inner transformation ultimately becomes a gift to the world because in becoming freely, simply, and naturally human, we lose all the reasons to dis-empower, manipulate, or control others. Instead of shrinking back from reality, we naturally embrace everything because it is recognized to be an extension of our own being. The experience of oneness with life is can be compared to a Divine Love affair. The feeling of deep Love, appreciation, and intimacy towards all of life ever deepens, and we settle into a deep and loving relationship with all of existence. Love cannot help but be devoted to all life, because it sees itself always wherever it looks.

As we transform our self into Divine-Human beings, we naturally align with the vibration of Love. As we continually uncover the source of lasting peace, and become more accepting of what is, it is only natural to collaborate harmoniously with the outer world. As a result; encouraging others, wanting to see all of humanity empowered, free, and happy becomes a natural expression of our Love. Serving the world is not seen as an effort, a mission, or a project, or even as a goal to be accomplished, but as an effortless extension and expression of our inner state.

The beauty of transformation and moving through all the stages of becoming

Freely-Human is that you are left with all of its totality right here and right now. All of life is fully available to you in every moment. The benefit to having gone through a full and complete integration and acceptance of the 'space suit' means you are now a naturally accepting Divine-Human, fully able to be present to life, to people, and free to hold all of its totality on all levels in each moment. Being comfortable and accepting of all aspects of the totality leads to an increased degree of tolerance towards the relationships in your life. Acceptance of pain, or 'negative' emotions within your inner space leads to a willingness to also be accepting of your friends and family during times of distress. Allow them the space and freedom to be exactly as they are, rooted in the certainty that they are perfect, even in this. Transformation gives us total freedom to be simply human without shrinking back from any of the experiences we face here. Each moment can be addressed and embraced with full presence of real being. Life can now be fully appreciated as the precious gift and fleeting miracle that it really is.

Practical application: 3-2-1 freely human meditation

This meditation is a combination of three of the most valuable practices I have found in my own process. These are: the 'allowing' practice, and the 'I don't know' practice, combined with bringing all of totality into the 'light of conscious awareness'.

- 3. Allow everything to be as it is, this moment, here and now. Allow yourself to also be; simply stop right now, and be exactly as you are.

- 2. Fall into the unconditioned mind, let yourself 'not know' what anything is, or what it all means.

- 1. Continue allowing, and not knowing, and simply hold everything, every single thing you are aware of in this moment, in the presence of total awareness. Hold everything as it is, without an agenda, and turn the light of conscious awareness on it.

- Hold all three together as one.

The reason I like to use the title 3-2-1 for this meditation is because you finish with the word 'one'. An amazing experiment is to practice the 3-2-1 meditation every morning for a week. Notice how your day changes; notice how your interactions with people and relationships are influenced when you see everyone through the lens of 'one' consciousness.

Clarification of terms

I don't speak from a particular tradition or lineage, but rather share what I have learned and tasted directly from my own process of transformation. My intention was to use words that are freeing and empowering for the reader, to inspire the direct experience of the liberated and limitless being within each of us. My goal was to create a book that is as neutral as possible in terms of tradition or religion, and instead to peel everything back to raw essence and then use the most universal words possible to point to that.

My wish is to take an approach to freedom and inner peace that the majority of people on our planet can relate to, regardless of their religious or philosophical background. I have tried to use terms that are spiritually neutral in hopes that the reader will insert or exchange my wording for the terminology that resonates for them the most. Because these Universal terms may be new to some readers, I have also included a section devoted to clarifying those that are used most frequently in this book.

Clarification of Terms from the story, 'It's Time:'

The Angels: The angels represent your Divine essence or eternal original nature as pure consciousness. Your eternal nature is already free and unbound.

Density: Everything we see in the world of form is a manifestation or a variation of one consciousness. Everything vibrates or fluctuates at different levels of frequency, some higher, some lower; the lower vibrating frequencies can feel unpleasant, foggy, heavy, unclear or dense. The frequency of Universal, unconditional, and causeless Love resonates closely with our original nature of pure consciousness. Pure consciousness was never bound; it is light, spacious and free.

The Space Suit: The space suit started out with a purpose, but forgetfulness, lack of clarity, and difference in density made the space suit eventually become a burden, an obstacle, and ultimately a cause of suffering and distress. The space suit represents our habitual unconscious tendencies, thoughts or fear-based patterns of behaviour.

The Space Suit Mask: The cloudy mask represents the mental preoccupation with the past and the future and how that inhibits us from seeing clearly.

Reflections in the Glass: This represents the unconscious or unaware aspects of our self that we have repressed or rejected. These reflections are then superimposed on the world around us, and because they are forgotten we see them reflected on the world and assume that we are seeing the full picture. An example to illustrate this: imagine that someone is walking into your house with a serious expression on their face. You have been feeling upset about something but have not had a chance to process it and are mentally preoccupied with something else. Because you are not fully conscious of your unprocessed emotion, you see that particular emotional energy superimposed on the person's face, and assume that you know what the person is feeling. In reality, the person may be completely preoccupied with their own issues and not even aware of you being in the room.

The Angels up Above: These represent our Divine guidance system, our natural intelligence, or our direct link to Divine qualities of inner wisdom, insight and inspiration.

Other Clarification of Terms:

Essence: Our original essence which is eternal, formless, limitless and unable to be harmed.

Separation: The identification or preoccupation with thoughts, ideas, unconsciousness, fear or lack, leading to the belief that we are separate from our eternal nature, from life, and from each other.

Freely-Human: A term used interchangeably with Divinely-Human. When we are no longer identified with thoughts, or perceive ourselves as a limited individual, we become rooted in our liberated nature of pure and eternal consciousness. As this consciousness is interwoven with our physical form we embody the full potential of being a conscious human being united and connected to all other humans and all of life.

Divinely-Human: A term used interchangeably with Freely-Human. When we are no longer identified with thoughts, or perceive ourselves as a limited individual, we become rooted in our liberated nature of pure and eternal consciousness. As this consciousness is interwoven with our physical form we embody the full potential of being a conscious human being united and connected to all other humans and all of life.

Unconscious Thought: An aspect of mind (see below) or the space suit.

Cultural conditioning: The set of conditions we place on feeling whole, complete, or happy. This is reinforced by our cultures messages of influence. Take, for example, advertising: when we agree with the messages of happiness being conditional, the weight of that agreement is carried into our behaviour and plays out in the world.

Inspired or Higher Thought: An aspect of natural intelligence (see below).

Love: Love as it is used in this book is an aspect of our eternal nature. The true nature of Love has no opposite; it cannot be contained or owned, and is universally unconditional. This is not the same as emotional or romantic love.

Frequency: The technical definition of the word 'frequency' is *the rate at which something occurs or is repeated over a particular period of time or in a given sample.* In this book I am referring to frequency in order to help the reader peel back form to the see the rate at which the energy is vibrating. The word 'frequency', in this book, is often referred to in relation to a thought, feeling or sensation. At the deepest level, everything we see in the world of form is energy, and these energies we see all vibrate at different frequencies. When we can pan back, and see form from the level of pure frequency, it temporarily removes our mental labels so that we can see it in a new light.

Consciousness: The term 'consciousness' is used to point to our eternal nature as Divine beings.

Awareness: Awareness can be used interchangeably with the term 'consciousness' in this book; awareness is what is left when all else falls away.

The Shadow: The term 'shadow' can be used interchangeably with the reflections on the glass as illustrated in the story, 'It's Time'. Shadows and reflections point to the aspects of our mind and consciousness of which we are not consciously aware.

Integration: Integration is just another way to say re-unite. To integrate is to merge with, embrace or welcome all aspects of life. By holding pain or discomfort in the arms of Love we welcome it back in and dissolve the walls of separation around it. If you think of the aspects of life that you dislike as being a crying baby, you wouldn't want to throw the baby on the floor; you would want to pick it up and hold it with Love. This is the way we also integrate and re-unite with life. After some time of Love and acceptance, we no longer feel at the mercy of life or apart from it, as we are one with all.

Clear Seeing: Seeing with clarity was illustrated in the story, 'It's Time' when the Angel was first able to see clearly through her mask. Through deep acceptance of what is, and applying the power of conscious awareness to our experience of the present moment, we can see things from beyond the lens of our conditioned or unconscious patterns of thought, behaviour or preprogrammed ideas of how we 'should' be. Clear seeing enables us to be fully present and receptive to life as it is, and available to the planet, humanity, and the experience of life.

Conscious Choice: When we are seeing clearly and consciously and are rooted in present moment awareness, we can make an empowered choice as an extension of our inner state. When we are preoccupied with seeking and defending, we are not seeing clearly and, as a result, choices we make are an extension of the unconscious thoughts and limiting beliefs.

Mind: The term 'mind' is used to highlight the aspect of the mind that represents unconscious thinking, ideas about the past and future, rationalizing, justifying, defending, claiming personal ownership, unhealthy judgment, and other mental functions motivated by separation that isolate us as separate individuals. The mind in this context can be used interchangeably with the space suit and its reflections. While there is also a higher aspect of mind that governs inspired thought, creative genius, and thoughts that flow from the essence of one eternal consciousness, for the purpose of making a clear distinction, in this book, the higher aspects of mind are referred to as *natural intelligence* or *the unconditioned mind.*

Natural Intelligence: The higher aspect of mind that governs inspired thought, creative genius, and thoughts that flow from the essence of one eternal consciousness. Natural intelligence is impersonal, unlimited, unconditional, and inherently liberated.

The Unconditioned Mind: The aspect of mind that is unconditioned and has not bought into the social agreements of placing conditions on Love or happiness. An example of the unconditioned mind is the innocence and purity of a newborn baby.

Acknowledgements

This book has been a collaboration of many souls who share a beautiful vision; it has been an honor to be part of such a harmonious and gifted team. It is not possible to name everyone, but I want to express my gratitude to the few who deserve special mention. First, I would like to thank the dedicated members at Inner Splendor Media: my publisher, Vidura Barrios, for your presence and unwavering intention to serve from the heart, and also Kanta Barrios and Jeffrey Main for all your endless hours of effort, wisdom, and kindness.

I would like to thank my editors: Justin Phillips for your ability to always stay in synch with the message, Namdev Hayes for your depth of insight in bringing this book to its full potential, and Margaret Bendet for your final revisions to the text and your much needed and appreciated refinements.

I thank my many friends and family members for your helpful suggestions, generous time, and guidance as well as for always providing space for me to be human. Especially, my gratitude goes to Kim Marr, Kerri Taylor, Karen McPhee, Ryan and Tracy Phillips, Mikael Hedman, Elizabeth Churchill, Vanessa Taylor, Jennifer Kozak, Susan Wolf, David Montgomery, Kevin Corlette, Keith Doll, Giampaolo Ferradini, Shaila Reddy, Todd Strong, Sam Chahda, Jamie Romkey, Joanne Mercier, and my many other supporters who continue to encourage the integrity of this message. I would also like to mention my yoga students and clients, for your sincere questions are the reason this book exists. A special thanks also goes to the dolphins for reuniting me with the excitement of being alive.

I offer a heartfelt thank you to my parents, Arthur and Dianne Wushke, and my sister, Jennifer Wushke, for your encouragement to do what I can to make the world a better place and for your ongoing support and generosity; and to my son, Evan, whose natural wisdom inspires me every day.

And I extend a very special thank you to my wonderful teacher, Karam Guirgis, who shone the light on what I really am so I could remember it for myself.

To everyone who has been a part of the creation of this book and to the readers, thank you; it is deeply inspiring to witness the growing numbers awakening each day to the joy of being freely human.

Author Biography

Christine Wushke is a certified hatha yoga and meditation teacher with almost two decades of practice and a commitment to assisting students. Christine's goal as a teacher is to inspire students to experience the divine stillness, the unutterable peace, that is within each human being. Having realized her own inner truth, she empowers others to realize theirs.

Christine's teaching is also available on DVD: *Easy Yoga for Beginners* and the *Ocean of Light* guided meditation CD series. For more information on Christine, including her book tour schedule, please visit www.FreedomIsYourNature.com.